GOOD TIDINGS OF GREAT JOY

Good Tidings of Great Joy

The Birth of Jesus the Messiah

WILLIAM BARCLAY

Westminster John Knox Press
Louisville, Kentucky

Book design by Sharon Adams
Cover design by Jennifer K. Cox
Cover photograph © 1999 PhotoDisc, Inc.

First edition
Published by Westminster John Knox Press
Louisville, Kentucky

This book is printed on acid-free paper that meets
the American National Standards Institute Z39.48 standard. ♾

PRINTED IN THE UNITED STATES OF AMERICA
99 00 01 02 03 04 05 06 07 08— 10 9 8 7 6 5 4 3 2 1

A catalog card for this book may be obtained from the Library of Congress

ISBN 0-664-25850-6

Contents

Introduction

"Let us go now to Bethlehem and see this thing that has taken place, which the Lord has made known to us."

The celebration of Christmas is a special time of the year, full of gatherings and gift giving. For most, Christmas is special also as a time to remember the event that changed human history, the coming of God in Jesus Christ. Each year in the days of December, many set aside time for contemplation and preparation for the arrival (again) of the Savior into their lives.

The readings of this book are drawn from William Barclay's Daily Study Bible. For many years, Barclay's profound insights have inspired readers. Now this collection shares his thoughts on the Gospel passages about the birth of the Messiah. Arranged as daily devotions, these reflections allow the reader to travel the road to Bethlehem, to hear the praise of angels, to follow the Magi, and to worship the baby in the manger who is also the Lord of Creation.

In some faith traditions, the seasons of Advent, Christmas, and Epiphany provide a structure to help anticipate this joyous event. This book is conceived with an eye toward those traditions, but is also sensitive that many can benefit from daily readings without that structure. *Good Tidings of Great Joy* is designed for personal use, family gatherings, and group Bible studies. Its easy-to-use format allows for reading and rereading year after year.

The significance of the coming of Jesus cannot be overstated. That God would enter into and join with humanity says much about both the sacredness of life and the nature of God. In Barclay's words,

"What Jesus did was to open a window in time that we might see the eternal and unchanging love of God." It is my hope that these devotions might point to that window, and help each of us prepare in our journey to meet the Christ child. In the words of Luke 2:15, may we too "see this great thing which the Lord has made known to us."

                                                    Chris Conver

In the Beginning Was the Word

NOVEMBER 29

The Word Became Flesh

John 1:1–5

When the world had its beginning, the Word was already there; and the Word was with God; and the Word was God. This Word was in the beginning with God. He was the agent through whom all things were made; there is not a single thing which exists in this world which came into being without him. In him was life and the life was the light of men; and the light shines in the darkness, because the darkness has never been able to conquer it.

The first chapter of the Fourth Gospel is one of the greatest adventures of religious thought ever achieved by the mind of man.

It was not long before the Christian church was confronted with a very basic problem. It had begun in Judaism. In the beginning all its members had been Jews. By human descent Jesus was a Jew, and, to all intents and purposes, except for brief visits to the districts of Tyre and Sidon, and to the Decapolis, he was never outside Palestine. Christianity began amongst the Jews; and therefore inevitably it spoke in the Jewish language and used Jewish categories of thought.

But although it was cradled in Judaism it very soon went out into the wider world. Within thirty years of Jesus' death it had travelled all over Asia Minor and Greece and had arrived in Rome. By A.D. 60 there must have been a hundred thousand Greeks in the church for every Jew who was a Christian. Jewish ideas were completely strange to the Greeks. To take but one outstanding example, the Greeks had never heard of the Messiah. The very centre of Jewish expectation, the coming of the Messiah, was an idea that was quite alien to the Greeks. The very category in which the Jewish Christians conceived and presented Jesus meant nothing to them. Here then was the problem— how was Christianity to be presented to the Greek world?

Lecky, the historian, once said that the progress and spread of any idea depends not only on its strength and force but on the predisposition to receive it of the age to which it is presented. The task of the Christian church was to create in the Greek world a predisposition to receive the Christian message. As E. J. Goodspeed put it, the question was, "Must a Greek who was interested in Christianity be routed through Jewish Messianic ideas and through Jewish ways of thinking, or could some new approach be found which would speak out of his background to his mind and heart?" The problem was how to present Christianity in such a way that a Greek would understand.

Round about the year A.D. 100 there was a man in Ephesus who was fascinated by that problem. His name was John. He lived in a Greek city. He dealt with Greeks to whom Jewish ideas were strange and unintelligible and even uncouth. How could he find a way to present Christianity to these Greeks in a way that they would welcome and understand? Suddenly the solution flashed upon him. In both Greek and Jewish thought there existed the conception of *the word.* Here was something which could be worked out to meet the double world of Greek Jew. Here was something which belonged to the heritage of both races and that both could understand.

Let us then begin by looking at the two backgrounds of the conception of *the word.*

NOVEMBER 30

The Jewish Background

John 1:1
When the world had its beginning, the Word was already there; and the Word was with God; and the Word was God.

In the Jewish background four strands contributed something to the idea of *the word.*

(i) To the Jew a word was far more than a mere sound; it was something which had an independent existence and which actually did things. As Professor John Paterson has put it: "The spoken word to the Hebrew was fearfully alive. . . . It was a unit of energy charged with power. It flies like a bullet to its billet." For that very reason the

Hebrew was sparing of words. Hebrew speech has fewer than 10,000; Greek speech has 200,000.

When John Knox preached in the days of the Reformation in Scotland it was said that the voice of that one man put more courage into the hearts of his hearers than ten thousand trumpets braying in their ears. His words did things to people. In the days of the French Revolution Rouget de Lisle wrote the *Marseillaise* and that song sent men marching to revolution. The words did things. In the days of the Second World War, when Britain was bereft alike of allies and of weapons, the words of the Prime Minister, Sir Winston Churchill, as he broadcast to the nation, did things to people.

It was even more so in the East, and still is. To the Eastern people a word is not merely a sound; it is power which does things. Once when Sir George Adam Smith was travelling in the desert in the East, a group of Moslems gave his party the customary greeting: "Peace be upon you." At the moment they failed to notice that he was a Christian. When they discovered that they had spoken a blessing to an infidel, they hurried back to ask for the blessing back again. The word was like a thing which could be sent out to do things and which could be brought back again. Will Carleton, the poet, expresses something like that:

> Boys flying kites haul in their white-winged birds;
> You can't do that way when you're flying words:
> "Careful with fire," is good advice we know,
> "Careful with words," is ten times doubly so.
> Thoughts unexpressed may sometimes fall back dead,
> But God himself can't kill them when they're said.

We can well understand how to the Eastern peoples words had an independent, power-filled existence.

(ii) Of that general idea of the power of words, the Old Testament is full. Once Isaac had been deceived into blessing Jacob instead of Esau, nothing he could do could take that word of blessing back again (Genesis 27). The word had gone out and had begun to act and nothing could stop it. In particular we see the word of God in action in the

Creation story. At every stage of it we read: "And God said . . ." (Genesis 1:3, 6, 11). The word of God is the creating power. Again and again we get this idea of the creative, acting, dynamic word of God. "By the word of the Lord the heavens were made" (Psalm 33:6). "He sent forth his word and healed them" (Psalm 107:20). "He sent forth his commands to the earth; his word runs swiftly" (Psalm 147:15). "So shall my word be that goes forth from my mouth; it shall not return to me empty, but it shall accomplish that which I purpose, and prosper in the thing for which I sent it" (Isaiah 55:11). "Is not my word like fire, and, says the Lord, like a hammer which breaks the rock in pieces?" (Jeremiah 23:29). Everywhere in the Old Testament there is this idea of the powerful, creative word. Even men's words have a kind of dynamic activity; how much more must it be so with God?

(iii) There came into Hebrew religious life something which greatly accentuated the development of this idea of the word of God. For a hundred years and more before the coming of Jesus Hebrew was a forgotten language. The Old Testament was written in Hebrew but the Jews no longer knew the language. The scholars knew it, but not the ordinary people. They spoke a development of Hebrew called Aramaic, which is to Hebrew somewhat as modern English is to Anglo-Saxon. Since that was so the scriptures of the Old Testament had to be translated into this language that the people could understand, and these translations were called the Targums. In the synagogue the scriptures were read in the original Hebrew, but then they were translated into Aramaic and Targums were used as translations.

The Targums were produced in a time when men were fascinated by the transcendence of God and could think of nothing but the distance and the difference of God. Because of that the men who made the Targums were very much afraid of attributing human thoughts and feelings and actions to God. To put it in technical language, they made every effort to avoid *anthropomorphism* in speaking of him.

Now the Old Testament regularly speaks of God in a human way; and wherever they met a thing like that the Targums substituted the *word of God* for the name of God. Let us see how this custom worked. In Exodus 19:17 we read that "Moses brought the people out of the camp *to meet God.*" The Targums thought that was too human a way to speak of God, so they said that Moses brought the people out of the camp to meet the *word of God.* In Exodus 31:13 we read that God said to the people that the Sabbath "is a sign between me and you throughout your generations." That was far too human a way to speak for the Targums, and so they said that the Sabbath is a sign "between *my word* and you." Isaiah 48:13 has a great picture of creation: "My hand laid the foundation of the earth, and my right hand spread out the heavens." That was much too human a picture of God for the Targums and they made God say: "By *my word* I have founded the earth; and by my strength I have hung up the heavens."

(iv) At this stage we must look more fully at something we already began to look at in the introduction. The Greek term for *word* is *Logos;* but *Logos* does not only mean *word;* it also means *reason.* For John, and for all the great thinkers who made use of this idea, these two meanings were always closely intertwined. Whenever they used *Logos* the twin ideas of the word of God and the reason of God were in their minds.

The Jews had a type of literature called the wisdom literature, which was the concentrated wisdom of sages. It is not usually speculative and philosophical, but practical wisdom for the living and management of life. In the Old Testament the great example of wisdom literature is the book of Proverbs. In this book there are certain passages which give a mysterious life-giving and eternal power to Wisdom (Sophia). In these passages Wisdom has been, as it were, personified, and is thought of as the eternal agent and co-worker of God. There are three main passages.

The first is Proverbs 3:13–26. Out of that passage we may specially note:

> She is a tree of *life* to those who lay hold of her; those who hold her fast are called happy. *The Lord by wisdom* founded the earth; by understanding he established the heavens; by his knowledge the deeps broke forth, and the clouds drop down the dew. (Proverbs 3:18–20)

We remember that *Logos* means *word* and also means *reason.* We have already seen how the Jews thought of the powerful and creative word of God. Here we see the other side beginning to emerge. *Wisdom* is God's agent in enlightenment and in creation; and *wisdom* and *reason* are very much the same thing. We have seen how important *Logos* was in the sense of *word;* now we see it beginning to be important in the sense of *wisdom* or *reason.*

The second important passage is Proverbs 4:5–13. In it we may notice:

> Keep hold of instruction, do not let go; guard her, for she is your life.

The *word* is the *light* of men and *wisdom* is the *light* of men. The two ideas are amalgamating with each other rapidly now. The most important passage of all is in Proverbs 8:1–9:2. In it we may specially note:

> The Lord created me [Wisdom is speaking] at the beginning of his work, the first of his acts of old. Ages ago I was set up, at the first, before the beginning of the earth. When there were no depths I was brought forth, when there were no springs abounding with water. Before the mountains had been shaped, before the hills, I was brought forth; before he had made the earth with its fields, or the first of the dust of the world. When he established the heavens, I was there, when he drew a circle on the face of the deep; when he made firm the skies above; when he established the fountains of the deep; when he assigned to the sea its limit, so that the waters might not transgress his command; when he marked out the foundations of the earth, then I was beside him, like a master workman; and I was daily his delight, rejoicing before him always. (Proverbs 8:22–30)

When we read that passage there is echo after echo of what John says of the *word* in the first chapter of his Gospel. *Wisdom* had that eternal existence, that light-giving function, that creative power which John attributed to the *word,* the *Logos,* with which he identified Jesus Christ.

So when John was searching for a way in which he could commend Christianity he found in his own faith and in the record of his own people the idea of the *word,* the ordinary word which is in itself not merely a sound, but a dynamic thing, the *word* of God by which God created the world, the *word* of the Targums which expressed the very idea of the action of God. So John said: "If you wish to see that *word* of God, if you wish to see the creative power of God, if you wish to see that *word* which brought the world into existence and which gives light and life to every man, *look at Jesus Christ.* In him the *word* of God came among you."

DECEMBER 1

The Greek Background

John 1:1 (continued)
When the world had its beginning, the Word was already there; and the Word was with God; and the Word was God.

We began by seeing that John's problem was not that of presenting Christianity to the Jewish world, but of presenting it to the Greek world. How then did this idea of the *word* fit into Greek thought? It was already there waiting to be used. In Greek thought the idea of the *word* began away back about 560 B.C., and, strangely enough, in Ephesus where the Fourth Gospel was written.

In 560 B.C. there was an Ephesian philosopher called Heraclitus whose basic idea was that everything is in a state of flux. Everything was changing from day to day and from moment to moment. His famous illustration was that it was impossible to step twice into the same river. You step into a river; you step out; you step in again; but you do not step into the same river, for the water has flowed on and it is a different river. To Heraclitus everything was like that; everything was in a constantly changing state of flux. But if that be so, why was life not complete chaos? How can there be any sense in a world where there was constant flux and change?

The answer of Heraclitus was: all this change and flux was not haphazard; it was controlled and ordered, following a continuous pattern all the time; and that which controlled the pattern was the *Logos,* the *word,* the *reason* of God. To Heraclitus, the *Logos* was the principle of order under which the universe continued to exist. Heraclitus went further. He held that not only was there a pattern in the physical world; there was also a pattern in the world of events. He held that nothing moved with aimless feet; in all life and in all the events of life there was a purpose, a plan and a design. And what was it that controlled events? Once again, the answer was *Logos.*

Heraclitus took the matter even nearer home. What was it that in us individually told us the difference between right and wrong? What made us able to think and to reason? What enabled us to choose aright and to recognize the truth when we saw it? Once again Heraclitus gave the same answer. What gave a man reason and knowledge of the truth and the ability to judge between right and wrong was the *Logos* of God dwelling within him. Heraclitus held that in the world of nature and events "all things happen according to the *Logos,*" and that in the individual man "the *Logos* is the judge of truth." The *Logos* was nothing less than the mind of God controlling the world and every man in it.

Greek thought knew all about the *Logos;* it saw in the *Logos* the creating and guiding and directing power of God, the power which made the universe and kept it going. So John came to the Greeks and said: "For centuries you have been thinking and writing and dreaming about the *Logos,* the power which made the world, the power which keeps the order of the world, the power by which men think and reason and know, the power by which men come into contact with God. Jesus is that *Logos* come down to earth." "The Word," said John, "became flesh." We could put it another way—"The mind of God became a person."

Both Jew And Greek

Slowly the Jews and Greeks had thought their way to the conception of the *Logos,* the mind of God which made the world and makes sense of it. So John went out to Jews and Greeks to tell them that in Jesus Christ this creating, illuminating, controlling, sustaining mind of

God had come to earth. He came to tell them that men need no longer guess and grope; all that they had to do was to look at Jesus and see the mind of God.

DECEMBER 2

The Eternal Word

John 1:1–2

When the world had its beginning, the Word was already there; and the Word was with God; and the Word was God. This Word was in the beginning with God.

The beginning of John's Gospel is of such importance and of such depth of meaning that we must study it almost verse by verse. It is John's great thought that Jesus is none other than God's creative and life-giving and light-giving *word,* that Jesus is the power of God which created the world and the reason of God which sustains the world come to earth in human and bodily form.

Here at the beginning John says three things about the *word;* which is to say that he says three things about Jesus.

(i) The *word* was already there at the very beginning of things. John's thought is going back to the first verse of the Bible. "In the beginning God created the heavens and the earth" (Genesis 1:1). What John is saying is this—the *word* is not one of the created things; the *word* was there *before creation.* The *word* is not part of the world which came into being in time; the *word* is part of eternity and was there with God before time and the world began. John was thinking of what is known as *the pre-existence of Christ.*

In many ways this idea of pre-existence is very difficult, if not altogether impossible, to grasp. But it does mean one very simple, very practical, and very tremendous thing. If the *word* was with God before time began, if God's word is part of the eternal scheme of things, it means that *God was always like Jesus.* Sometimes we tend to think of God as stern and avenging; and we tend to think that something Jesus did changed God's anger into love and altered his attitude to men. The New Testament knows nothing of that idea. The whole

New Testament tells us, this passage of John especially, that God has always been like Jesus. What Jesus did was to open a window in time that we might see the eternal and unchanging love of God.

We may well ask, "What then about some of the things that we read in the Old Testament? What about the passages which speak about commandments of God to wipe out whole cities and to destroy men, women and children? What of the anger and the destructiveness and the jealousy of God that we sometimes read of in the older parts of Scripture?" The answer is this—it is not God who has changed; it is men's knowledge of him that has changed. Men wrote these things because they did not know any better; that was the stage which their knowledge of God had reached.

When a child is learning any subject, he has to learn it stage by stage. He does not begin with full knowledge; he begins with what he can grasp and goes on to more and more. When he begins music appreciation, he does not start with a Bach Prelude and Fugue; he starts with something much more simple, and goes through stage after stage until his knowledge grows. It was that way with men and God. They could only grasp and understand God's nature and his ways in part. It was only when Jesus came that they saw fully and completely what God has *always* been like.

It is told that a little girl was once confronted with some of the more bloodthirsty and savage parts of the Old Testament. Her comment was: "But that happened before God became a Christian!" If we may so put it with all reverence, when John says that the *word* was always there, he is saying that God was always a Christian. He is telling us that God was and is and ever shall be like Jesus; but men could never know and realize that until Jesus came.

(ii) John goes on to say that *the Word was with God*. What does he mean by that? He means that always there has been the closest connection between the *word* and God. Let us put that in another and a simpler way—there has always been the most intimate connection between Jesus and God. That means no one can tell us what God is like, what God's will is for us, what God's love and heart and mind are like, as Jesus can.

Let us take a simple human analogy. If we want to know what someone really thinks and feels about something, and if we are unable to approach the person ourselves, we do not go to someone who is merely an acquaintance of that person, to someone who has known him only a short time; we go to someone whom we know to be an intimate friend of many years' standing. We know that he will really be able to interpret the mind and the heart of the other person to us.

It is something like that that John is saying about Jesus. He is saying that Jesus has always been with God. Let us use every human language because it is the only language we can use. John is saying that Jesus is so intimate with God that God has no secrets from him; and that, therefore, Jesus is the one person in all the universe who can reveal to us what God is like and how God feels towards us.

(iii) Finally John says that *the Word was God.* This is a difficult saying for us to understand, and it is difficult because Greek, in which John wrote, had a different way of saying things from the way in which English speaks. When Greek uses a noun it almost always uses the definite article with it. The Greek for God is *theos* and the definite article is *ho.* When Greek speaks about God it does not simply say *theos;* it says *ho theos.* Now when Greek does not use the definite article with a noun that noun becomes much more like an adjective. John did not say that the *word* was *ho theos;* that would have been to say that the *word* was *identical* with God. He said that the *word* was *theos*—without the definite article—which means that the *word* was, we might say, of the very same character and quality and essence and being as God. When John said *the Word was God* he was not saying that Jesus was identical with God; he was saying that Jesus was so perfectly the same as God in mind, in heart, in being that in him we perfectly see what God is like.

So right at the beginning of his Gospel John lays it down that in Jesus, and in him alone, there is perfectly revealed to men all that God always was and always will be, and all that he feels towards and desires for men.

DECEMBER 3

The Creator of All Things

John 1:3
He was the agent through whom all things were made; and there is not a single thing which exists in this world which came into being without him.

It may seem strange to us that John so stresses the way in which the world was created; and it may seem strange that he so definitely connects Jesus with the work of creation. But he had to do this because of a certain tendency in the thought of his day.

In the time of John there was a kind of heresy called *Gnosticism*. Its characteristic was that it was an intellectual and philosophical approach to Christianity. To the Gnostics the simple beliefs of the ordinary Christian were not enough. They tried to construct a philosophic system out of Christianity. They were troubled about the existence of sin and evil and sorrow and suffering in this world, so they worked out a theory to explain it. The theory was this.

In the beginning two things existed—the one was God and the other was matter. Matter was always there and was the raw material out of which the world was made. The Gnostics held that this original matter was flawed and imperfect. We might put it that the world got off to a bad start. It was made of material which had the seeds of corruption in it.

The Gnostics went further. God, they said, is pure spirit, and pure spirit can never touch matter at all, still less matter which is imperfect. Therefore it was not possible for God to carry out the work of creation himself. So he put out from himself a series of emanations. Each emanation was further and further away from God and as the emanations got further and further away from him, they knew less and less about him. About halfway down the series there was an emanation which knew nothing at all about God. Beyond that stage the emanations began to be not only ignorant of but actually hostile to God. Finally in the series there was an emanation which was so distant from God that it was totally ignorant of him and totally hostile to him—and that emanation was the power which created the world, because it was so distant from God that it was possible for it to touch this flawed and evil matter. The creator god was utterly divorced from and utterly at enmity with the real God.

The Gnostics took one step further. They identified the creator god with the God of the Old Testament; and they held that the God of the Old Testament was quite different from, quite ignorant of and quite hostile to the God and Father of Jesus Christ.

In the time of John this kind of belief was widespread. Men believed that the world was evil and that an evil God had created it. It is to combat this teaching that John here lays down two basic Christian truths. In point of fact the connection of Jesus with creation is repeatedly laid down in the New Testament, just because of this background of thought which divorced God from the world in which we live. In Colossians 1:16 Paul writes: "For in him all things were created, in heaven and on earth . . . all things were created through him and for him." In First Corinthians 8:6 he writes of the Lord Jesus Christ "through whom are all things." The writer to the Hebrews speaks of the one who was the Son, "through whom also God created the world" (Hebrews 1:2). John and the other New Testament writers who spoke like this were stressing two great truths.

(i) Christianity has always believed in what is called *creation out of nothing*. We do not believe that in his creation of the world God had to work with alien and evil matter. We do not believe that the world began with an essential flaw in it. We do not believe that the world began with God and something else. It is our belief that behind everything there is God and God alone.

(ii) Christianity has always believed that this is *God's world*. So far from being so detached from the world that he could have nothing to do with it, God is intimately involved in it. The Gnostics tried to put the blame for the evil of the world on the shoulders of its creator. Christianity believes that what is wrong with the world is due to man's sin. But even though sin has injured the world and kept it from being what it might have been, we can never despise the world, because it is essentially God's. If we believe this it gives us a new sense of the value of the world and a new sense of responsibility to it.

There is a story of a child from the back streets of a great city who was taken for a day in the country. When she saw the bluebells in the woods, she asked: "Do you think God would mind if I picked some of his flowers?" This is God's world; because of that nothing is out of his control; and because of that we must use all things in the awareness that they belong to God. The Christian does not belittle the world by thinking that it was created by an ignorant and a hostile god; he glorifies it by remembering that everywhere God is behind it and in it. He believes that the Christ who re-creates the world was the co-worker of God when the world was first created, and that, in the act of redemption, God is seeking to win back that which was always his own.

DECEMBER 4

Life and Light

John 1:4
In him was life and the life was the light of men.

In a great piece of music the composer often begins by stating the themes which he is going to elaborate in the course of the work. That is what John does here. *Life* and *light* are two of the great basic words on which the Fourth Gospel is built up. They are two of the main themes which it is the aim of the Gospel to develop and to expound. Let us look at them in detail.

The Fourth Gospel begins and ends with *life*. At the very beginning we read that in Jesus was *life;* and at the very end we read that John's aim in writing the Gospel was that men might "believe that Jesus is the Christ, the Son of God, and that believing you may have *life* in his name" (John 20:31). The word is continually on the lips of Jesus. It is his wistful regret that men will not come to him that they might have *life* (5:40). It is his claim that he came that men might have *life* and that they might have it abundantly (10:10). He claims that he gives men *life* and that they will never perish because no one will snatch them out of his hand (10:28). He claims that he is the way, the truth and the *life* (14:6). In the Gospel the word *life* (*zoe*) occurs more than thirty-five times and the verb *to live* or *to have life* (*zen*) more than fifteen times. What then does John mean by *life?*

(i) Quite simply he means that *life* is the opposite of destruction, condemnation, and death. God sent his Son that the man who believes should not perish but have eternal *life* (3:16). The man who hears and believes has eternal *life* and will not come into judgment (5:24). There is a contrast between the resurrection to *life* and the resurrection to *judgment* (5:29). Those to whom Jesus gives *life* will never perish (10:28). There is in Jesus that which gives a man security in this life and in the life to come. Until we accept Jesus and take him as our saviour and enthrone him as our king we cannot be said to live at all. The man who lives a Christless life *exists,* but he does not know what *life* is. Jesus is the one person who can make life worth living, and in whose company death is only the prelude to fuller life.

(ii) But John is quite sure that, although Jesus is the bringer of this *life,* the giver of life is God. Again and again John uses the phrase *the living God,* as indeed the whole Bible does. It is the will of the Father who sent Jesus that everyone who sees him and believes on him should have life (6:40). Jesus is the giver of life because the Father has set his own seal of approval upon him (6:27). He gives life to as many as God has given him (17:2). At the back of it all there is God. It is as if God was saying: "I created men that they should have real life; through their sin they have ceased to live and only exist; I have sent them my Son to enable them to know what real life is."

(iii) We must ask what this life is. Again and again the Fourth Gospel uses the phrase *eternal life.* The word John uses for *eternal* is *aionios.* Clearly whatever else *eternal* life is, it is not simply life which lasts for ever. A life which lasted for ever could be a terrible curse; often the thing for which men long is release from life. In eternal life there must be more than *duration* of life; there must be a certain *quality* of life.

Life is not desirable unless it is a certain kind of life. Here we have the clue. *Aionios* is the adjective which is repeatedly used to describe God. In the true sense of the word *only* God is *aionios, eternal;* therefore *eternal life is that life which God lives.* What Jesus offers us from God is God's own life. Eternal life is life which knows something of the serenity and power of the life of God himself. When Jesus came offering men *eternal life,* he was inviting them to enter into the very life of God.

(iv) How, then, do we enter into that life? We enter into it *by believing in Jesus Christ.* The word *to believe* (*pisteuein*) occurs in the Fourth Gospel no fewer than seventy times. "He who believes in the Son has eternal life" (3:36). "He who believes," says Jesus, "has eternal life" (6:47). It is God's will that men should see the Son, and believe in him, and have eternal life (5:24). What does John mean by *to believe?* He means two things.

(*a*) He means that we must be convinced that Jesus is really and truly the Son of God. He means that we must make up our minds about him. After all, if Jesus is only a man, there is no reason why we should give him the utter and implicit obedience that he demands. We have to think out for ourselves who he was. We have to look at him, learn about him, study him, think about him until we are driven to the conclusion that this is none other than the Son of God.

(*b*) But there is more than intellectual belief in this. To believe in Jesus means to take Jesus at his word, to accept his commandments as absolutely binding, to believe without question that what he says is true.

For John, belief means the conviction of the mind that Jesus is the Son of God, the trust of the heart that everything he says is true and the basing of every action on the unshakable assurance that we must take him at his word. When we do that we stop existing and begin living. We know what *Life* with a capital *L* really means.

DECEMBER 5

Life and Light

John 1:4
In him was life and the life was the light of men.

The second of the great Johannine key-words which we meet here is the word *light.* This word occurs in the Fourth Gospel no fewer than twenty-one times. Jesus is the *light* of men. The function of John the Baptist was to point men to that *light* which was in Christ. Twice Jesus calls himself the *light* of the world (8:12; 9:5). This *light* can be in men (11:10), so that they can become children of the *light* (12:36); "I have come," said Jesus, "as light into the world" (12:46). Let us see if we can understand something of this idea of the *light* which Jesus brings into the world. Three things stand out.

(i) The *light* Jesus brings is the *light* which puts chaos to flight. In the creation story God moved upon the dark, formless chaos which was before the world began and said: "Let there be light" (Genesis 1:3). The new-created light of God routed the empty chaos into which it came. So Jesus is *the light which shines in the darkness* (1:5). He is the one person who can save life from becoming a chaos. Left to ourselves we are at the mercy of our passions and our fears.

When Jesus dawns upon life, light comes. One of the oldest fears in the world is the fear of the dark. There is a story of a child who was to sleep in a strange house. His hostess, thinking to be kind, offered to leave the light on when he went to bed. Politely he declined the offer. "I thought," said his hostess, "that you might be afraid of the dark." "Oh, no," said the lad, "you see, it's God's dark." With Jesus the night is light about us as the day.

(ii) The *light* which Jesus brings is a revealing *light.* It is the condemnation of men that they loved the darkness rather than the *light;* and they did so because their deeds were evil; and they hated the *light* lest their deeds should be exposed (3:19, 20). The *light* which Jesus brings is something which shows things as they are. It strips away the disguises and the concealments; it shows things in all their nakedness; it shows them in their true character and their true values.

Long ago the Cynics said that men hate the truth for the truth is like the light to sore eyes. In Caedmon's poem there is a strange picture. It is a picture of the last day and in the centre of the scene there is the cross; and from the cross there flows a strange blood-red light, and the mysterious quality of that light is such that it shows things as they are. The externals, the disguises, the outer wrappings and trappings are stripped away; and everything stands revealed in the naked and awful loneliness of what it essentially is.

We never see ourselves until we see ourselves through the eyes of Jesus. We never see what our lives are like until we see them in the light of Jesus. Jesus often drives us to God by revealing us to ourselves.

(iii) The *light* which Jesus brings is a guiding *light*. If a man does not possess that *light* he walks in darkness and does not know where he is going (12:36). When a man receives that *light* and believes in it, he walks no more in darkness (12:46). One of the features of the Gospel stories which no one can miss is the number of people who came running to Jesus asking: "What am I to do?" When Jesus comes into life the time of guessing and of groping is ended, the time of doubt and uncertainty and vacillation is gone. The path that was dark becomes light; the decision that was wrapped in a night of uncertainty is illumined. Without Jesus we are like men groping on an unknown road in a black-out. With him the way is clear.

DECEMBER 6

The Hostile Dark

John 1:5
And the light shines in the darkness, and the darkness did not put it out.

Here we meet another of John's key-words—*darkness* (*skotos, skotia*). This word occurs seven times in the Gospel. To John there was a *darkness* in the world that was as real as the *light*.

(i) The *darkness* is hostile to the *light*. The light shines in the *darkness,* but, however hard the *darkness* tries, it cannot extinguish it. Sinning man loves the *darkness* and hates the light, because the light shows up too many things.

It may well be that in John's mind there is a borrowed thought here. John, as we know, was prepared to go out and to take in new ideas, if by so doing he could present and commend the Christian message to men. The great Persian religion of Zoroastrianism had at this time a very great influence on men's thoughts. It believed that there were two great opposing powers in the universe, the god of the light and the god of the dark, Ahriman and Ormuzd. This whole universe was a battleground in the eternal, cosmic conflict between the light and the dark; and all that mattered in life was the side a man chose.

So John is saying: "Into this world there comes Jesus, the light of the world; there is a darkness which would seek to eliminate him, to banish him from life, to extinguish him. But there is a power in Jesus that is undefeatable. The darkness can hate him, but it can never get rid of him." As has been truly said: "Not all the darkness in the world can extinguish the littlest flame." The unconquerable light will in the end defeat the hostile dark. John is saying: "Choose your side in the eternal conflict and choose aright."

(ii) The *darkness* stands for the natural sphere of all those who hate the good. It is men whose deeds are evil who fear the light (3:19, 20). The man who has something to hide loves the dark; but it is impossible to hide anything from God. His searchlight sweeps the shadows and illuminates the skulking evils of the world.

(iii) There are certain passages where the *darkness* seems to stand for *ignorance,* especially for that wilful ignorance which refuses the light of Jesus Christ. Jesus says: "I am the light of the world; he who follows me will not walk in *darkness*" (8:12). He says to his disciples that the light will be with them only for so short a time; let them walk in it; if they do not, the *darkness* comes and a man who walks in *darkness* does not know where he is going (12:35). He says that he came with his light that men should not abide in *darkness* (12:46). Without Jesus Christ a man cannot find or see the way. He is like a blindfolded man or even a blind man. Without Jesus Christ life goes lost. It was Goethe who cried out for: "Light, more light!" It was one of the old Scots leaders who said to his friends towards the end: "Light the candle that I may see to die." Jesus is the light which shows a man the road, and which lights the road at every step of the way.

There are times when John uses this word *darkness* symbolically. He uses it at times to mean more than merely the dark of an earthly night. He tells of Jesus walking on the water. He tells how the disciples had embarked on their boat and were crossing the lake without

Jesus; and then he says, "*And it was now dark,* and Jesus had not yet come to them" (6:17). Without the presence of Jesus there was nothing but the threatening dark. He tells of the Resurrection morning and of the hours before those who had loved Jesus realized that he had risen from the dead. He begins the story: "Now on the first day of the week Mary Magdalene came, *while it was still dark*" (20:1). She was living at the moment in a world from which she thought Jesus had been eliminated, and a world like that was dark. He tells the story of the Last Supper. He tells how Judas received the sop and then went out to do his terrible work and arrange for the betrayal of Jesus; and he says with a kind of terrible symbolism: "So, after receiving the morsel, he immediately went out; *and it was night*" (13:30). Judas was going out into the night of a life which had betrayed Christ.

To John the Christless life was life in the dark. The *darkness* stands for life without Christ, and especially for that which has turned its back on Christ.

Before we leave this passage there is one other thing to note. The word which we have translated *put out* is in Greek *katalambanein.* This word can have three meanings.

(*a*) It can mean that the darkness never *understood* the light. There is a sense in which the man of the world simply cannot understand the demands of Christ and the way Christ offers him. To him it seems sheer foolishness. A man cannot understand Christ until he first submits to him.

(*b*) It can mean the darkness never *overcame* the light. *Katalambanein* can mean *to pursue until one overtakes and so lays hold on and overcomes.* This could mean that the darkness of the world had done everything possible to eliminate Jesus Christ, even to crucifying him, but it could never destroy him. This could be a reference to the crucified and conquering Christ.

(*c*) It can be used of *extinguishing a fire or flame.* That is the sense in which we have taken it here. Although men did all they could to obscure and extinguish the light of God in Christ, they could not quench it. In every generation the light of Christ still shines in spite of the efforts of men to extinguish the flame.

And the Word Became Flesh

DECEMBER 7

The Light of Every Man

John 1:9

He was the real light, who, in his coming into the world, gives light to every man.

In this verse John uses a very significant word to describe Jesus. He says that Jesus was the *real* light. In Greek there are two words which are very like each other. The Authorized Version and the Revised Standard use the word *true* to translate both of them; but they have different shades of meaning. The first is *alethes*. *Alethes* means *true* as opposed to *false;* it is the word that would be used of a statement which is true. The other word is *alethinos*. *Alethinos* means *real* or *genuine* as opposed to unreal.

So what John is saying is that Jesus is the real light come to illumine men. Before Jesus came there were other lights which men followed. Some were flickers of the truth; some were faint glimpses of reality; some were will o' the wisps which men followed and which led them out into the dark and left them there. It is still the case. There are still the partial lights; and there are still the false lights; and men still follow them. Jesus is the only genuine light, the real light to guide men on their way.

John says that Jesus, by his coming into the world, brought the real light to men. His coming was like a blaze of light. It was like the coming of the dawn. A traveller tells how once in Italy he was standing on a hill overlooking the Bay of Naples. It was so dark that nothing could be seen; then all a sudden there came a lightning flash and everything, in every detail, was lit up. When Jesus came into this world he came like a light in the dark.

(i) His coming dissipated the shadows of *doubt.* Until he came men could only guess about God. "It is difficult to find out about God," said one of the Greeks, "and when you have found out about him it is impossible to tell anyone else about him." To the pagan, God either dwelt in the shadows that no man can penetrate or in the light that no man can approach. But when Jesus came men saw full-displayed what God is like. The shadows and the mists were gone; the days of guessing were at an end; there was no more need for a wistful agnosticism. The light had come.

(ii) His coming dissipated the shadows of *despair*. Jesus came to a world that was in despair. "Men," as Seneca said, "are conscious of their helplessness in necessary things." They were longing for a hand let down to help them up. "They hate their sins but cannot leave them." Men despaired of ever making themselves or the world any better. But with the coming of Jesus a new power came into life. He came not only with knowledge but with power. He came not only to show them the right way but to enable them to walk in it. He gave them not only instruction but a presence in which all the impossible things had become possible. The darkness of pessimism and despair was gone for ever.

(iii) His coming dissipated the darkness of *death*. The ancient world feared death. At the best, death was annihilation and the soul of man shuddered at the thought. At the worst, it was torture by whatever gods there be and the soul of man was afraid. But Jesus by his coming, by his life, his death, his Resurrection showed that death was only the way to a larger life. The darkness was dispelled. Stevenson has a scene in one of his stories in which he draws the picture of a young man who has almost miraculously escaped in a duel in which he was certain he would be killed. As he walks away his heart is singing: "The bitterness of death is past." Because of Jesus the bitterness of death is past for every man.

Further, Jesus is the light who lights *every* man who comes into the world. The ancient world was exclusive. The Jew hated the Gentile and held that Gentiles were created for no other purpose than to be fuel for the fires of hell. True, there was a lonely prophet who saw that Israel's destiny was to be a light to the Gentiles (Isaiah 42:6; 49:6), but that was a destiny which Israel had always definitely refused. The Greek world never dreamed that knowledge was for every man. The Roman world looked down on the barbarians, the lesser breeds without the law. But Jesus came to be a light to *every* man. Only the God and Father of our Lord Jesus Christ has a heart big enough to hold all the world.

DECEMBER 8

Unrecognized

John 1:10–11

He was in the world, and, although the world came into being through him, the world did not recognize him. It was into his own home that he came, and his own people did not welcome him.

When John wrote this passage two thoughts were in his mind.

(i) He was thinking of the time before Jesus Christ came into the world in the body. From the beginning of time God's *Logos* has been active in the world. In the beginning God's creating, dynamic *word* brought the world into being; and ever since it is the *word,* the *Logos,* the *reason* of God which has made the world an ordered whole and man a thinking being. If men had only had the sense to see him, the *Logos* was always recognizable in the universe.

The Westminster Confession of Faith begins by saying that "the lights of nature, and the works of creation and providence do so far manifest the goodness, wisdom and power of God as to leave men inexcusable." Long ago Paul had said that the visible things of the world were so designed by God as to lead men's thoughts to the invisible things, and that if men had looked with open eyes and an understanding heart at the world their thoughts would have been inevitably led to the creator of the world (Romans 1:19, 20). The world has always been such that, looked at in the right way, it would lead men's minds to God.

Theology has always made a distinction between *natural* theology and *revealed* theology. Revealed theology deals with the truths that came to us directly from God in the words of the prophets, the pages of his book, and supremely in Jesus Christ. Natural theology deals with the truths that man could discover by the exercise of his own mind and intellect on the world in which he lives. How, then, can we see God's *word,* God's *Logos,* God's *reason,* God's *mind* in the world in which we live?

(*a*) We must look *outwards.* It was always a basic Greek thought that where there is order there must be a mind. When we look at the world we see an amazing order. The planets keep to their appointed courses. The tides observe their appointed times. Seed times and harvest, summer and winter, day and night come in their appointed order. Clearly there is order in nature, and, therefore, equally clearly there must be a mind behind it all. Further, that mind must be greater than any human mind because it achieves results that the human mind can never achieve. No man can make day into night, or night into day; no man can make a seed that will have in it the power of growth; no man can make a living thing. If in the world there is order, there must be mind; and if in that order there are things which are beyond the mind of man to do, then the mind behind the order of nature must be a mind above and beyond the mind of man—and straightway we have reached God. To look outwards upon the world is to come face to face with the God who made it.

(*b*) We must look *upwards*. Nothing demonstrates the amazing order of the universe so much as the movement of the world. Astronomers tell us that there are as many stars as there are grains of sand upon the seashore. If we may put it in human terms, think of the traffic problem of the heavens; and yet the heavenly bodies keep their appointed courses and travel their appointed way. An astronomer is able to forecast to the minute and to the inch when and where a certain planet will appear. An astronomer can tell us when and where an eclipse of the sun will happen hundreds of years from now, and he can tell us to the second how long it will last. It has been said that "no astronomer can be an atheist." When we look upwards we see God.

(*c*) We must look *inwards*. Where did we get the power to think, to reason, and to know? Where did we get our knowledge of right and of wrong? Why does even the most evil-ridden man know in his heart of hearts when he is doing a wrong thing? Kant said long ago that two things convinced him of the existence of God—the starry heavens above him and the moral law within him. We neither gave ourselves life, nor did we give ourselves the reason which guides and directs life. It must have come from some power outside ourselves. Where do remorse and regret and the sense of guilt come from? Why can we never do what we like and be at peace? When we look inwards we find what

Marcus Aurelius called "the god within," and what Seneca called "the holy spirit which sits within our souls." No man can explain himself apart from God.

(*d*) We must look *backwards*. Froude, the great historian, said that the whole of history is a demonstration of the moral law in action. Empires rise and empires collapse. As Kipling wrote:

> Lo, all our pomp of yesterday
> Is one with Nineveh and Tyre!

And it is a demonstrable fact of history that moral degeneration and national collapse go hand in hand. "No nation," said George Bernard Shaw, "has ever outlived the loss of its gods." All history is the practical demonstration that there is a God.

So, then, even if Jesus Christ had never come into this world in bodily form, it would still have been possible for men to see God's *word,* God's *Logos,* God's *reason* in action. But, although the action of the *word* was there for all to see, men never recognized him.

DECEMBER 9

Unrecognized

John 1:10–11 (continued)

He was in the world, and, although the world came into being through him, the world did not recognize him. It was into his own home that he came, and his own people did not welcome him.

(ii) In the end God's creating and directing *word* did come into this world in the form of the man Jesus. John says that the *word* came to his own home and his own people gave him no welcome. What does he mean by that? He means that when God's *word* entered this world, he did not come to Rome or to Greece or to Egypt or to the Eastern Empires. *He came to Palestine;* Palestine was specially God's land and the Jews were specially God's people.

The very titles by which the Old Testament calls the land and the people show that. Palestine is called the *holy land* (Zechariah 2:12). It is called *the Lord's land;* God speaks of it as *his land* (Hosea 9:3;

Jeremiah 2:7; 16:18; Leviticus 25:23). The Jewish nation is called *God's peculiar treasure* (Exodus 19:5; Psalm 135:4). The Jews are called *God's special people* (Deuteronomy 7:6). They are called God's *peculiar people* (Deuteronomy 14:2; 26:18). They are called *the Lord's portion* (Deuteronomy 32:9).

Jesus came to a land which was peculiarly God's land and a people who were peculiarly God's people. He ought, therefore, to have been coming to a nation that would welcome him with open arms; the door should have been wide open for him; he should have been welcomed like a wayfarer coming home; or, even more, like a king coming to his own—but *he was rejected.* He was received with hate and not with adoration.

Here is the tragedy of a people being prepared for a task and then refusing that task. It may be that parents plan and save and sacrifice to give a son or a daughter a chance in life, to prepare that son or daughter for some special task and opportunity—and then when the chance comes, the one for whom so much sacrifice was made refuses to grasp the opportunity, or fails miserably when confronted with the challenge. Therein is tragedy. And that is what happened to God.

It would be wrong to think that God prepared only the Jewish people. God is preparing every man and woman and child in this world for some task that he has in store for them. A novelist tells of a girl who refused to touch the soiling things of life. When she was asked why, she said: "Some day something fine is going to come into my life, and I want to be ready for it." The tragedy is that so many people refuse the task God has for them.

We may put it in another way—a way that strikes home—there are so few people who become what they have it in them to be. It may be through lethargy and laziness; it may be through timidity and cowardice; it may be through lack of discipline and self-indulgence; it may be through involvement in second-bests and byways; but the world is full of people who have never realized the possibilities which are in them. We need not think of the task God has in store for us in terms of some great act or achievement of which all men will know. It may be to fit a child for life; it may be at some crucial moment to

speak that word and exert that influence which will stop someone ru-
ining his life; it may be to do some quite small job superlatively well;
it may be to touch the lives of many by our hands, our voices, or our
minds. The fact remains that God is preparing us by all the experi-
ences of life for *something;* and many refuse the task when it comes
and never even realize that they are refusing it.

There is all the pathos in the world in the simple saying: "He came
to his own home—and his own people gave him no welcome." It happened to Jesus long ago—and it is happening yet.

DECEMBER 10

Children of God

John 1:12–13

*To all those who did receive him, to those who believe in his name, he
gave the right to become the children of God. These were born not of
blood, nor of any human impulse, nor of any man's will, but their birth
was of God.*

Not everyone rejected Jesus when he came; there were some who did
receive him and welcome him; and to them Jesus gave the right to become children of God.

There is a sense in which a man is not naturally a child of God.
There is a sense in which he has to *become* a child of God. We may
think of this in human terms, because human terms are the only ones
open to us.

There are two kinds of sons. There is the son who never does anything else but use his home. All through his youth he takes everything
that the home has to offer and gives nothing in return. His father may
work and sacrifice to give him his chance in life, and he takes it as a
right, never realizing what he is taking and making no effort to de-
serve it or repay it. When he leaves home, he makes no attempt to
keep in touch. The home has served his purpose, and he is finished
with it. He realizes no bond to be maintained and no debt to be paid.
He is his father's son; to his father he owes his existence; and to his father he owes what he is; but between him and his father there is no

bond of love and intimacy. The father has given all in love; but the son has given nothing in return.

On the other hand there is the son who all his life realizes what his father is doing and has done for him. He takes every opportunity to show his gratitude by trying to be the son his father would wish him to be; as the years go on he grows closer and closer to his father; the relationship of father and son becomes the relationship of fellowship and friendship. Even when he leaves home the bond is still there, and he is still conscious of a debt that can never be repaid.

In the one case the son grows further and further away from the father; in the other he grows nearer and nearer the father. Both are sons, but the sonship is very different. The second has *become* a son in a way that the first never was.

We may illustrate this kind of relationship from another, but a kindred, sphere. The name of a certain younger man was mentioned to a famous teacher, whose student the younger man claimed to be. The older man answered: "He may have attended my lectures, but he was not one of my students." There is a world of difference between sitting in a teacher's class room and being one of his students. There can be contact without communion; there can be relationship without fellowship. All men are the sons of God in the sense that they owe to him the creation and the preservation of their lives; but only some men *become* the sons of God in the depth and intimacy of the true father and son relationship.

It is the claim of John that men can enter into that true and real sonship only through Jesus Christ. When he says that it does not come from blood, he is using Jewish thought, for the Jews believed that a physical son was born from the union of the seed of the father with the blood of the mother. This sonship does not come from any human impulse or desire or from any act of the human will; it comes entirely from God. We cannot make ourselves sons of God; we have to enter into a relationship which God offers us. No man can ever enter into friendship with God by his own will and power; there is a great gulf fixed between the human and the divine. Man can only enter into friendship with God when God himself opens the way.

Again let us think in human terms. A commoner cannot approach a king with the offer of friendship; if there is ever to be such a friendship it must depend entirely on the approach of the king. It is so with us and God. We cannot by will or achievement enter into fellowship with God, for we are men and he is God. We can enter into it only when God in his totally undeserved grace condescends to open the way to himself.

But there is a human side to this. What God offers, man has to appropriate. A human father may offer his son his love, his advice, his friendship, and the son may refuse it and prefer to take his own way. It is so with God; God offers us *the right* to become sons but we need not accept it.

We do accept it through believing in the name of Jesus Christ. What does that mean? Hebrew thought and language had a way of using *the name* which is strange to us. By that expression Jewish thought did not so much mean the name by which a person was called as his nature in so far as it was revealed and known. For instance, in Psalm 9:10 the psalmist says: "Those who know *thy name* put their trust in thee." Clearly that does not mean that those who know that God is called Jehovah will trust him; it means that those who know God's character, God's nature, who know what God is like, will be ready and willing to trust him for everything. In Psalm 20:7 the psalmist says: "Some boast of chariots and some of horses: but we boast of *the name* of the Lord our God." Clearly that does not mean that we will boast that God is called Jehovah. It means that some people will put their trust in human aids, but we will put our trust in God because we know what he is like.

To trust in the name of Jesus therefore means to put our trust in what he is. He was the embodiment of kindness and love and gentleness and service. It is John's great central doctrine that in Jesus we see the very mind of God, the attitude of God to men. If we believe that, then we also believe that God is like Jesus, as kind, as loving as Jesus was. To believe in the name of Jesus is to believe that God is like him; and it is only when we believe that, that we can submit ourselves to God and become his children. Unless we had seen in Jesus what God is like we would never even have dared to think of ourselves as being able to become the children of God. It is what Jesus is that opens to us the possibility of becoming the children of God.

DECEMBER 11

The Word Became Flesh

John 1:14

So the Word of God became a person, and took up his abode in our being, full of grace and truth; and we looked with our own eyes upon his glory, glory like the glory which an only son receives from a father.

Here we come to the sentence for the sake of which John wrote his Gospel. He has thought and talked about the word of God, that powerful, creative, dynamic word which was the agent of creation, that guiding, directing, controlling word which puts order into the universe and mind into man. These were ideas which were known and familiar to both Jew and Greek. Now he says the most startling and incredible thing that he could have said. He says quite simply: "This word which created the world, this reason which controls the order of the world, has become a person and with our own eyes we saw him." The word that John uses for *seeing* this word is *theasthai;* it is used in the New Testament more than twenty times and is always used of *actual physical sight.* This is no spiritual vision seen with the eye of the soul or of the mind. John declares that the word actually came to earth in the form of a man and was seen by human eyes. He says: "If you want to see what this creating word, this controlling reason, is like, look at Jesus of Nazareth."

This is where John parted with all thought which had gone before him. This was the entirely new thing which John brought to the Greek world for which he was writing. Augustine afterwards said that in his pre-Christian days he had read and studied the great pagan philosophers and had read many things, but he had never read that the word became flesh.

To a Greek this was the impossible thing. The one thing that no

Greek would ever have dreamed of was that God could take a body. To the Greek the body was an evil, a prison-house in which the soul was shackled, a tomb in which the spirit was confined. Plutarch, the wise old Greek, did not even believe that God could control the happenings of this world directly; he had to do it by deputies and intermediaries, for, as Plutarch saw it, it was nothing less than blasphemy to involve God in the affairs of the world. Philo could never have said it. He said: "The life of God has not descended to us; nor has it come as far as the necessities of the body." The great Roman Stoic Emperor, Marcus Aurelius, despised the body in comparison with the spirit. "Therefore despise the flesh-blood and bones and a net-work, a twisted skein of nerves and veins and arteries." "The composition of the whole body is under corruption."

Here was the shatteringly new thing—that God could and would become a human person, that God could enter into this life that we live, that eternity could appear in time, that somehow the Creator could appear in creation in such a way that men's eyes could actually see him.

So staggeringly new was this conception of God in a human form that it is not surprising that there were some even in the church who could not believe it. What John says is that the word became *sarx*. Now *sarx* is the very word Paul uses over and over again to describe what he called *the flesh,* human nature in all its weakness and in all its liability to sin. The very thought of taking this word and applying it to God was something that their minds staggered at. So there arose in the church a body of people called *Docetists.*

Dokein is the Greek word for *to seem to be.* These people held that Jesus in fact was only a phantom; that his human body was not a real body; that he could not really feel hunger and weariness, sorrow and pain; that he was in fact a disembodied spirit in the apparent form of a man. John dealt with these people much more directly in his First Letter. "By this you know the Spirit of God: every spirit which confesses that Jesus Christ has come *in the flesh* is of God, and every spirit which does not confess Jesus is not of God. This is the spirit of Antichrist" (1 John 4:2, 3). It is true that this heresy was born of a kind of mistaken reverence which recoiled from saying that Jesus was really, fully, and truly human. To John it contradicted the whole Christian gospel.

It may well be that we are often so eager to conserve the fact that Jesus was fully God that we tend to forget the fact that he was fully man. *The Word became flesh*—here, perhaps as nowhere else in the New Testament, we have the full manhood of Jesus gloriously proclaimed. In Jesus we see the creating word of God, the controlling reason of God, taking manhood upon himself. In Jesus we see God living life as he would have lived it if he had been a man. Supposing we said nothing else about Jesus we could still say that he shows us how God would live this life that we have to live.

DECEMBER 12

The Word Became Flesh

John 1:14

So the Word of God became a person, and took up his abode in our being, full of grace and truth; and we looked with our own eyes upon his glory, glory like the glory which an only son receives from a father.

It might well be held that this is the greatest single verse in the New Testament; we must therefore spend much time upon it so that we may enter the more fully into its riches.

We have already seen how John has certain great words which haunt his mind and dominate his thought and are the themes out of which his whole message is elaborated. Here we have three more of these words.

(i) The first is *grace*. This word has always two basic ideas in it.

(*a*) It always has the idea of something completely undeserved. It always has the idea of something that we could never have earned or achieved for ourselves. The fact that God came to earth to live and to die for men is not something which humanity deserved; it is an act of pure love on the part of God. The word grace emphasizes at one and the same time the helpless poverty of man and the limitless kindness of God.

(*b*) It always has the idea of beauty in it. In modern Greek the word means *charm*. In Jesus we see the sheer winsomeness of God.

Men had thought of God in terms of might and majesty and power and judgment. They had thought of the power of God which could crush all opposition and defeat all rebellion; but in Jesus men are confronted with the sheer loveliness of God.

(ii) The second is *truth*. This word is one of the dominant notes of the Fourth Gospel. We meet it again and again. Here we can only briefly gather together what John has to say about Jesus and the truth.

(*a*) Jesus is the embodiment of the truth. He said: "I am the truth" (14:6). To see truth we must look at Jesus. Here is something infinitely precious for every simple mind and soul. Very few people can grasp abstract ideas; most people think in pictures. We could think and argue for ever, and we would very likely be no nearer arriving at a definition of beauty. But if we can point at a beautiful person and say that *is* beauty, the thing becomes clear. Ever since men began to think about God they have been trying to define just who and what he is—and their puny minds get no nearer a definition. But we can cease our thinking and look at Jesus Christ and say: "That is what God is like." Jesus did not come to *talk* to men about God; he came to *show* men what God is like, so that the simplest mind might know him as intimately as the mind of the greatest philosopher.

(*b*) Jesus is the communicator of the truth. He told his disciples that if they continued with him they would know the truth (8:31). He told Pilate that his object in coming into this world was to witness to the truth (18:37). Men will flock to a teacher or preacher who can really give them guidance for the tangled business of thinking and living. Jesus is the one who, amidst the shadows, makes things clear; who, at the many crossroads of life, shows us the right way; who, in the baffling moments of decision, enables us to choose aright; who, amidst the many voices which clamour for our allegiance, tells us what to believe.

(*c*) Even when Jesus left this earth in the body, he left us his Spirit to guide us into the truth. His Spirit is the Spirit of truth (14:17; 15:26; 16:13). He did not leave us only a book of instruction and a body of teaching. We do not need to search through some unintelligible textbook to find out what to do. Still, to this day, we can ask Jesus what to do, for his Spirit is with us every step of the way.

(*d*) The truth is what makes us free (8:32). There is always a certain liberating quality in the truth. A child often gets queer, mistaken notions about things when he thinks about them himself; and often he becomes afraid. When he is told the truth he is emancipated from his fears. A man may fear that he is ill; he goes to the doctor; even if the verdict is bad he is at least liberated from the vague fears which haunted his mind. The truth which Jesus brings liberates us from estrangement from God; it liberates us from frustration; it liberates us from our fears and weaknesses and defeats. Jesus Christ is the greatest liberator on earth.

(*e*) The truth can be resented. They sought to kill Jesus because he told them the truth (8:40). The truth may well condemn a man; it may well show him how far wrong he was. "Truth," said the Cynics, "can be like the light to sore eyes." The Cynics declared that the teacher who never annoyed anyone never did anyone any good. Men may shut their ears and their minds to the truth; they may kill the man who tells them the truth—but the truth remains. No man ever destroyed the truth by refusing to listen to the voice that told it to him; and the truth will always catch up with him in the end.

(*f*) The truth can be disbelieved (8:45). There are two main reasons why men disbelieve the truth. They may disbelieve it because it seems too good to be true; or they may disbelieve it because they are so fastened to their half-truths that they will not let them go. In many instances a half-truth is the worst enemy of a whole truth.

(*g*) The truth is not something abstract; it is something which must be done (3:21). It is something which must be known with the mind, accepted with the heart, and acted out in the life.

DECEMBER 13

The Word Became Flesh

John 1:14

So the Word of God became a person, and took up his abode in our being, full of grace and truth; and we looked with our own eyes upon his glory, glory like the glory which an only son receives from a father.

A life-time of study and thought could not exhaust the truth of this verse. We have already looked at two of the great theme words in it; now we look at the third—*glory*. Again and again John uses this word in connection with Jesus Christ. We shall first look at what John says about the glory of Christ, and then we shall go on to see if we can understand a little of what he means.

(i) The life of Jesus Christ was a manifestation of glory. When he performed the miracle of the water and the wine at Cana of Galilee, John says that he manifested forth his glory (2:11). To look at Jesus and to experience his power and love was to enter into a new glory.

(ii) The glory which he manifests is the glory of God. It is not from men that he receives it (5:41). He seeks not his own glory but the glory of him who sent him (7:18). It is his Father who glorifies him (8:50, 54). It is the glory of God that Martha will see in the raising of Lazarus (11:4). The raising of Lazarus is for the glory of God, that the Son may be glorified thereby (11:4). The glory that was on Jesus, that clung about him, that shone through him, that acted in him is the glory of God.

(iii) Yet that glory was uniquely his own. At the end he prays that God will glorify him with the glory that he had before the world began (17:5). He shines with no borrowed radiance; his glory is his and his by right.

(iv) The glory which is his he has transmitted to his disciples. The glory which God gave him he has given to them (17:22). It is as if Jesus shared in the glory of God and the disciple shares in the glory of Christ. The coming of Jesus is the coming of God's glory among men.

What does John mean by all this? To answer that we must turn to the Old Testament. To the Jew the idea of the *Shechinah* was very dear. The *Shechinah* means *that which dwells;* and it is the word used for the visible presence of God among men. Repeatedly in the Old Testament we come across the idea that there were certain times when God's glory was visible among men. In the desert, before the giving of the manna, the children of Israel "looked toward the wilderness, and, behold, the glory of the Lord appeared in the cloud" (Exodus 16:10). Before the giving of the Ten Commandments, "the glory of the Lord settled upon

Mount Sinai" (Exodus 24:16). When the Tabernacle had been erected and equipped, "the glory of the Lord filled the tabernacle" (Exodus 40:34). When Solomon's Temple was dedicated the priests could not enter in to minister "for the glory of the Lord filled the house of the Lord" (1 Kings 8:11). When Isaiah had his vision in the Temple, he heard the angelic choir singing that "the whole earth is full of his glory" (Isaiah 6:3). Ezekiel in his ecstasy saw "the likeness of the glory of the Lord" (Ezekiel 1:28). In the Old Testament the glory of the Lord came at times when God was very close.

The glory of the Lord means quite simply the presence of God. John uses a homely illustration. A father gives to his eldest son his own authority, his own honour. The heir apparent to the throne, the king's heir, is invested with all the royal glory of his father. It was so with Jesus. When he came to this earth men saw in him the splendour of God, and at the heart of that splendour was love. When Jesus came to this earth men saw the wonder of God, and the wonder was love. They saw that God's glory and God's love were one and the same thing. The glory of God is not that of a despotic Eastern tyrant, but the splendour of love before which we fall not in abject terror but lost in wonder, love and praise.

You Shall Bear a Son

DECEMBER 14
A Son Is Promised

Luke 1:5–25

In the time of Herod, the king of Judaea, there was a priest called Zacharias, who belonged to the section of Abia. His wife was also a direct descendant of Aaron and her name was Elizabeth. Both of them were good people before God, for they walked blamelessly in all the commandments and ordinances of the Lord. They had no child because Elizabeth was barren and both of them were far advanced in years. When he was acting as priest before God, when his section was on duty, in accordance with the custom of priestly duty, it fell to him by lot to go into the Temple of the Lord to burn the incense. The whole congregation of the people was praying outside at the hour when incense was offered. The angel of the Lord appeared to him, standing at the right side of the altar of incense. When Zacharias saw him he was deeply moved and awe fell upon him. The angel said to him, "Do not be afraid, Zacharias, because your request has been heard and your wife Elizabeth will bear you a son and you must call him by the name of John. You will have joy and exultation and many will rejoice at his birth. He will be great in God's sight; he must not drink wine or strong drink and, even from the time he is in his mother's womb, he will be filled with the Holy Spirit. He will turn many sons of Israel to the Lord their God; and he himself will go before his face in the spirit and the power of Elijah, to turn the hearts of the fathers to the children, and the disobedient to the wisdom of the just, to get ready a people prepared for the Lord." Zacharias said to the angel, "How will I know that this is going to happen? For I am an old man and my wife is far advanced in years." "I am Gabriel," the angel answered, "who stands before God, and I have been sent to speak to you and to tell you this good news. And—look you—you will be silent and unable to speak until the day these things happen, because you did not believe my words which will be fulfilled in their own time." The people were waiting for Zacharias and they were surprised that he was lingering so long in the Temple. When he came out he was not able to speak to them and they realized that he had seen a vision in the Temple. He kept making signs to them but he remained unable to speak. When the days of his time of service were completed he went away to his own home. After these days Elizabeth his wife conceived; and she hid herself for five months. "This is God's doing for me," she said, "when he looked upon me to take away my shame among men."

Zacharias, the central character in this scene, was a priest. He belonged to the section of Abia. Every direct descendant of Aaron was automatically a priest. That meant that for all ordinary purposes there were far too many priests. They were therefore divided into twenty-four sections. Only at the Passover, at Pentecost, and at the Feast of Tabernacles did all the priests serve. For the rest of the year each course served two periods of one week each. Priests who loved their work looked forward to that week of service above all things; it was the highlight of their lives.

A priest might marry only a woman of absolutely pure Jewish lineage. It was specially meritorious to marry a woman who was also a descendant of Aaron, as was Elizabeth, the wife of Zacharias.

There were as many as twenty thousand priests altogether and so there were not far short of a thousand in each section. Within the sections all the duties were allocated by lot. Every morning and evening sacrifice was made for the whole nation. A burnt offering of a male lamb, one year old, without spot or blemish was offered, together with a meat offering of flour and oil and a drink offering of wine. Before the morning sacrifice and after the evening sacrifice incense was burned on the altar of incense so that, as it were, the sacrifices might go up to God wrapped in an envelope of sweet-smelling incense. It was quite possible that many a priest would never have the privilege of burning incense all his life; but if the lot did fall on any priest that day was the greatest day in all his life, the day he longed for and dreamed of. On this day the lot fell on Zacharias and he would be thrilled to the core of his being.

But in Zacharias's life there was tragedy. He and Elizabeth were childless. The Jewish rabbis said that seven people were excommunicated from God, and the list began, "A Jew who has no wife, or a Jew who has a wife and who has no child." Childlessness was a valid ground for divorce. Not unnaturally Zacharias, even on his great day, was thinking of his personal and domestic tragedy and was praying about it. Then the wondrous vision came and the glad message that, even when hope was dead, a son would be born to him.

The incense was burned and the offering made in the inmost court of the Temple, the Court of the Priests. While the sacrifice was being made, the congregation thronged the next court, the Court of the Israelites. It was the privilege of the priest at the evening sacrifice to come to the rail between the two courts after the incense had been burned in order to bless the people. The people marvelled that Zacharias was so long delayed. When he came he could not speak and the people knew that he had seen a vision. So in a wordless daze of joy Zacharias finished his week's duty and went home; and then the message of God came true and Elizabeth knew she was going to have a child.

One thing stands out here. *It was in God's house that God's message came to Zacharias.* We may often wish that a message from God would come to us. In Shaw's play, *Saint Joan,* Joan hears voices from God. The Dauphin is annoyed. "Oh, your voices, your voices," he said, "Why don't the voices come to me? I am king not you." "They do come to you," said Joan, "but you do not hear them. You have not sat in the field in the evening listening for them. When the angelus rings you cross yourself and have done with it; but if you prayed from your heart, and listened to the thrilling of the bells in the air after they stop ringing, you would hear the voices as well as I do." Joan gave herself the chance to hear God's voice. Zacharias was in the Temple waiting on God. God's voice comes to those who listen for it—as Zacharias did—in God's house.

DECEMBER 15

God's Message to Mary

Luke 1:26–38

In the sixth month the angel Gabriel was sent from God to a town of Galilee called Nazareth, to a maiden who was betrothed to a man called Joseph, who belonged to the house of David. The maiden's name was Mary. He came in to her and said, "Greetings, most favoured one. The Lord is with you." She was deeply moved at this word and wondered what a greeting like that could mean. The angel said to her, "Do not be afraid, Mary, for you have found favour in God's sight. Look you—you will conceive and you will bear a son and you must call him by the name of Jesus. He will be great and he will be called the Son of the Most High; and the Lord God will give him the throne of David his father; and he will rule over the house of Jacob forever, and there will be no end to his kingdom." Mary said to the angel, "How can this be since I do not know a man?" The angel answered, "The Holy Spirit will come upon you and the Spirit of the Most High will overshadow you, and so the child who will be born will be called holy, the Son of God, and—look you—Elizabeth, too, your kinswoman has also conceived in her old age; and this is now the sixth month for her who is called barren, because there is nothing which is impossible with God." Mary said, "I am the Lord's servant. Whatever he says, I accept." And the angel went away from her.

Mary was betrothed to Joseph. Betrothal lasted for a year and was quite as binding as marriage. It could be dissolved only by divorce. Should the man to whom a girl was betrothed die, in the eyes of the law she was a widow. In the law there occurs the strange-sounding phrase, "a virgin who is a widow."

In this passage we are face to face with one of the great controversial doctrines of the Christian faith—the Virgin Birth. The church does not insist that we believe in this doctrine. Let us look at the reasons for and against believing in it, and then we may make our own decision.

There are two great reasons for accepting it.

(i) The literal meaning of this passage, and still more of Matthew 1:18–25, clearly is that Jesus was to be born of Mary without a human father.

(ii) It is natural to argue that if Jesus was, as we believe, a very special person, he would have a special entry into the world.

Now let us look at the things which may make us wonder if the story of the virgin birth is to be taken as literally as all that.

(i) The genealogies of Jesus both in Luke and in Matthew (Luke 3:23–38; Matthew 1:1–17) trace the genealogy of Jesus through *Joseph,* which is strange if Joseph was not his real father.

(ii) When Mary was looking for Jesus on the occasion that he lingered behind in the Temple, she said, "Your father and I have been looking for you anxiously" (Luke 2:48). The name *father* is definitely given by Mary to Joseph.

(iii) Repeatedly Jesus is referred to as Joseph's son (Matthew 13:55; John 6:42).

(iv) The rest of the New Testament knows nothing of the virgin birth. True, in Galatians 4:4 Paul speaks of Jesus as "born of woman." But this is the natural phrase for any mortal man (cp. Job 14:1; 15:14; 25:4).

But let us ask, "If we do not take the story of the virgin birth literally, how did it arise?" The Jews had a saying that in the birth of *every* child there are three partners—the father, the mother, and the Spirit of God. They believed that no child could ever be born without the Spirit. And it may well be that the New Testament stories of the birth of Jesus are lovely, poetical ways of saying that, even if he had a human father, the Holy Spirit of God was operative in his birth in a unique way.

In this matter we may make our own decision. It may be that we will desire to cling to the literal doctrine of the virgin birth; it may be that we will prefer to think of it as a beautiful way of stressing the presence of the Spirit of God in family life.

Mary's submission is a very lovely thing. "Whatever God says, I accept." Mary had learned to forget the world's commonest prayer—"Thy will be *changed*"—and to pray the world's greatest prayer—"Thy will be *done*."

DECEMBER 16
The Paradox of Blessedness
Luke 1:39–45
In those days Mary arose and went eagerly to the hill country, to a city of Judah, and went into the house of Zacharias and greeted Elizabeth. When Elizabeth heard Mary's greeting the babe leaped in her womb and Elizabeth was filled with the Holy Spirit, and she lifted up her voice with a great cry and said, "Blessed are you among women and blessed is the

fruit of your womb. Why has this been granted to me—that the mother of my Lord should come to me? For—look you—when the voice of your greeting came to my ears the babe in my womb leaped with exultation. Blessed is she who believed that the things spoken to her from the Lord would find their fulfilment."

This is a kind of lyrical song on the blessedness of Mary. Nowhere can we better see the paradox of blessedness than in her life. To Mary was granted the blessedness of being the mother of the Son of God. Well might her heart be filled with a wondering, tremulous joy at so great a privilege. Yet that very blessedness was to be a sword to pierce her heart. It meant that some day she would see her son hanging on a cross.

To be chosen by God so often means at one and the same time a crown of joy and cross of sorrow. The piercing truth is that God does not choose a person for ease and comfort and selfish joy but for a task that will take all that head and heart and hand can bring to it. *God chooses a man in order to use him.* When Joan of Arc knew that her time was short she prayed, "I shall only last a year; use me as you can." When that is realized, the sorrows and hardships that serving God may bring are not matters for lamentation; they are our glory, for all is suffered for God.

When Richard Cameron, the Covenanter, was caught by the dragoons they killed him. He had very beautiful hands and they cut them off and sent them to his father with a message asking if he recognized them. "They are my son's," he said, "my own dear son's. Good is the will of the Lord who can never wrong me or mine." The shadows of life were lit by the sense that they, too, were in the plan of God. A great Spanish saint prayed for his people, "May God deny you peace and give you glory." A great modern preacher said, "Jesus Christ came not to make life easy but to make men great."

It is the paradox of blessedness that it confers on a person at one and the same time the greatest joy and the greatest task in all the world.

DECEMBER 17
A Wondrous Hymn
Luke 1:46–56

And Mary said, "My soul magnifies the Lord, and my spirit has exulted in God, my Saviour, because he looked graciously on the humble estate of his servant. For—look you—from now on all generations shall call me blessed, for the Mighty One has done great things for me and his name is holy. His mercy is from generation to generation to those who fear him. He demonstrates his power with his arm. He scatters the proud in the plans of their hearts. He casts down the mighty from their seats of power. He exalts the humble. He fills those who are hungry with good things and he sends away empty those who are rich. He has helped Israel, his son, in that he has remembered his mercy—as he said to our fathers that he would—to Abraham and to his descendants forever."

Here we have a passage which has become one of the great hymns of the church—the *Magnificat*. It is saturated in the Old Testament, and is specially kin to Hannah's song of praise in First Samuel 2:1–10. It has been said that religion is the opiate of the people; but, as Stanley Jones said, "the *Magnificat* is the most revolutionary document in the world."

It speaks of three of the revolutions of God.

(i) *He scatters the proud in the plans of their hearts.* That is a *moral* revolution. Christianity is the death of pride. Why? Because if a man sets his life beside that of Christ it tears the last vestiges of pride from him.

Sometimes something happens to a man which with a vivid, revealing light shames him. O. Henry has a short story about a lad who was brought up in a village. In school he used to sit beside a girl and they were fond of each other. He went to the city and fell into evil ways. He became a pickpocket and a petty thief. One day he snatched an old lady's purse. It was clever work and he was pleased. And then he saw coming down the street the girl whom he used to know, still sweet with the radiance of innocence. Suddenly he saw himself for the cheap, vile thing he was. Burning with shame, he leaned his head against the cool iron of a lamp standard. "God," he said, "I wish I could die." He saw himself.

Christ enables a man to see himself. It is the deathblow to pride. The moral revolution has begun.

(ii) *He casts down the mighty—he exalts the humble.* That is a *social* revolution. Christianity puts an end to the world's labels and prestige.

Muretus was a wandering scholar of the Middle Ages. He was poor. In an Italian town he took ill and was taken to a hospital for waifs and strays. The doctors were discussing his case in Latin, never dreaming he could understand. They suggested that since he was such a worthless wanderer they might use him for medical experiments. He looked up and answered them in their own learned tongue, "Call no man worthless for whom Christ died."

When we have realized what Christ did for all men, it is no longer possible to speak about a *common* man. The social grades are gone.

(iii) *He has filled those who are hungry . . . those who are rich he has sent empty away.* That is an *economic* revolution. A non-Christian society is an acquisitive society where each man is out to amass as much as he can get. A Christian society is a society where no man dares to have too much while others have too little, where every man must get only to give away.

There is loveliness in the *Magnificat* but in that loveliness there is dynamite. Christianity begets a revolution in each man and revolution in the world.

DECEMBER 18

His Name Is John

Luke 1:57–66

When Elizabeth's time to bear the child was completed she brought forth a son. When her neighbours and kinsfolk heard that the Lord had shown great mercy to her they rejoiced with her. On the eighth day they went to circumcise the child and it was their intention to call him Zacharias after his father. But his mother said, "No; he must be called John." They said to her, "There is no one in your connection who is called by this name." They asked his father by signs by what name he wished him to be called. He asked for a writing tablet and wrote, "John is his name." Im-

mediately his mouth was opened and his tongue was loosed and he kept on praising God. And great awe fell upon all the neighbours, and all these events were talked about in all the hill country of Judaea; and all those who heard them kept them in their hearts and said, "What will this child turn out to be, for the hand of the Lord is with him?"

In Palestine the birth of a boy was an occasion of great joy. When the time of the birth was near at hand, friends and local musicians gathered near the house. When the birth was announced and it was a boy, the musicians broke into music and song, and there was universal congratulation and rejoicing. If it was a girl the musicians went silently and regretfully away! There was a saying, "The birth of a male child causes universal joy, but the birth of a female child causes universal sorrow." So in Elizabeth's house there was double joy. At last she had a child and that child was a son.

On the eighth day the boy was circumcised and received his name. Girls could be named any time within thirty days of their birth. In Palestine names were descriptive. They sometimes described a circumstance attending the birth as *Esau* and *Jacob* do (Genesis 25:25–26). They sometimes described the child. *Laban,* for instance, means *white* or *blonde.* Sometimes the child received the parental name. Often the name described the parents' joy. *Saul* and *Samuel,* for instance, both mean *asked for.* Sometimes the name was a declaration of the parents' faith. *Elijah* for instance, means *Jehovah is my God.* Thus in a time of Baal worship Elijah's parents asserted their faith in the true God.

Elizabeth, to the neighbours' surprise, said that her son must be called John and Zacharias indicated that that was also his desire. *John* is a shorter form of the name *Jehohanan,* which means *Jehovah's gift* or *God is gracious.* It was the name which God had ordered to be given to the child and it described the parent's gratitude for an unexpected joy.

It was the question of the neighbours and of all who had heard the amazing story, "What will this child turn out to be?" Every child is a bundle of possibilities. There was an old Latin schoolmaster who always bowed gravely to his class before he taught them. When he was asked why, he answered, "Because you never know what one of these lads will turn out to be." The entry of a child into a family is two things. First, it is the greatest privilege which life can offer a man and wife. It is something for which to thank God. Second, it is one of life's supreme responsibilities, for that child is a bundle of possibilities, and on parents and teachers depends how these possibilities will or will not be realized.

DECEMBER 19

A Father's Joy

Luke 1:67–80

His father Zacharias was filled with the Holy Spirit and prophesied like this: "Blessed be the Lord, the God of Israel, because he has graciously visited his people and wrought deliverance for them. He has raised the horn of salvation for us in the house of David, his servant—as long ago he said he would through the mouth of his holy prophets—even deliverance from our enemies and from the hand of all who hate us, in that he has shown mercy to us as he did to our fathers and has remembered his holy covenant, the pledge which he gave to Abraham our father, to grant to us that we, being delivered from the hands of our enemies, should fearlessly serve him, in holiness and righteousness before him, all our days. And you, child, shall be called the prophet of the Most High; for you will walk before the Lord to prepare his ways, in order to give the knowledge of salvation to his people together with forgiveness of their sins, through the mercy of our God, in which the dawn from on high has graciously visited us, to shine upon those who sit in darkness and in the shadow of death, and to direct our feet in the way of peace."

And the child grew and was strengthened by the Spirit; and he lived in the desert places until the day when he was displayed to Israel.

Zacharias had a great vision for his son. He thought of him as the prophet and the forerunner who would prepare the way of the Lord. All devout Jews hoped and longed for the day when the Messiah, God's anointed king, would come. Most of them believed that, before he came, a forerunner would announce his coming and prepare his way. The usual belief was that Elijah would return to do so (Malachi 4:5). Zacharias saw in his son the one who would prepare the way for the coming of God's king.

Verses 75–77 give a great picture of the steps of the Christian way.

(i) There is *preparation.* All life is a preparation to lead us to Christ. When Sir Walter Scott was young his aim was to be a soldier. An accident made him slightly lame and that dream had to be abandoned. He took to reading the old Scottish histories and romances and so became the master novelist. An old man said of him, "He was makin' himsell a' the time; but he didna ken maybe what he was about till years had passed." In life God is working all things together to bring us to Christ.

(ii) There is *knowledge.* It is the simple fact that men did not know what God was like until Jesus came. The Greeks thought of a passionless God, beyond all joy and sorrow, looking on men in calm unmoved detachment—no help there. The Jews thought of a demanding God, whose name was law and whose function was that of judge—nothing but terror there. Jesus came to tell that God was love, and in staggered amazement men could only say, "We never knew that God was like that." One of the great functions of the incarnation was to bring to men the knowledge of God.

(iii) There is *forgiveness.* We must be clear about one thing regarding forgiveness. It is not so much the remission of penalty as the restoration of a relationship. Nothing can deliver us from certain consequences of our sins; the clock cannot be put back; but estrangement from God is turned to friendship. The distant God is become near and the God we feared is become the lover of the souls of men.

(iv) There is *walking* in the ways of peace. *Peace* in Hebrew does not mean merely freedom from trouble; it means all that makes for a man's highest good; and through Christ a man is enabled to walk in the ways that lead to everything that means life, and no longer to all that means death.

Jesus the Messiah, the Son of David

DECEMBER 20

The Lineage of the King

Matthew 1:1–17

This is the record of the lineage of Jesus Christ, the son of David, the son of Abraham.

Abraham begat Isaac, and Isaac begat Jacob. Jacob begat Judah and his brothers. Judah begat Phares and Zara, whose mother was Thamar. Phares begat Esrom. Esrom begat Aram. Aram begat Aminadab. Aminadab begat Naasson. Naasson begat Salmon. Salmon begat Booz, whose mother was Rachab. Booz begat Obed, whose mother was Ruth. Obed begat Jesse. Jesse begat David, the king.

David begat Solomon, whose mother was Uriah's wife. Solomon begat Roboam. Roboam begat Abia. Abia begat Asaph. Asaph begat Josaphat. Josaphat begat Joram. Joram begat Ozias. Ozias begat Joatham. Joatham begat Achaz. Achaz begat Ezekias. Ezekias begat Manasses. Manasses begat Amos. Amos begat Josias. Josias begat Jechonias, and his brothers, in the days when the exile to Babylon took place.

After the exile to Babylon Jechonias begat Salathiel. Salathiel begat Zorobabel. Zorobabel begat Abioud. Abioud begat Eliakim. Eliakim begat Azor. Azor begat Zadok. Zadok begat Acheim. Acheim begat Elioud. Elioud begat Eleazar. Eleazar begat Matthan. Matthan begat Jacob. Jacob begat Joseph, the husband of Mary, who was the mother of Jesus, who is called the Christ.

From Abraham to David there were in all fourteen generations. From David to the exile to Babylon there were also fourteen generations. From the exile to Babylon to the coming of Christ there were also fourteen generations.

It might seem to a modern reader that Matthew chose an extraordinary way in which to begin his Gospel; and it might seem daunting to present right at the beginning a long list of names to wade through. But to a Jew this was the most natural, and the most interesting, and indeed the most essential way to begin the story of any man's life.

The Jews were exceedingly interested in genealogies. Matthew calls this *the book of the generation* (*biblos geneseos*) of Jesus Christ. That to the Jews was a common phrase; and it means the record of a man's lineage, with a few explanatory sentences, where such comment was necessary. In the Old Testament we frequently find lists of the *generations* of famous men (Genesis 5:1; 10:1; 11:10; 11:27). When Josephus, the great Jewish historian, wrote his own autobiography, he began it with his own pedigree, which, he tells us, he found in the public records.

The reason for this interest in pedigrees was that the Jews set the greatest possible store on purity of lineage. If in any man there was the slightest admixture of foreign blood, he lost his right to be called a Jew, and a member of the people of God. A priest, for instance, was bound to produce an unbroken record of his pedigree stretching back to Aaron; and, if he married, the woman he married must produce her pedigree for at least five generations back. When Ezra was reorganizing the worship of God, after the people returned from exile, and was setting the priesthood to function again, the children of Habaiah, the children of Koz, and the children of Barzillai were debarred from office, and were labeled as polluted because "these sought their registration among those enrolled in the genealogies, but they were not found there" (Ezra 2:62).

These genealogical records were actually kept by the Sanhedrin. Herod the Great was always despised by the pure-blooded Jews because he was half an Edomite; and we can see the importance that even Herod attached to these genealogies from the fact that he had the official registers destroyed, so that no one could prove a purer pedigree than his own. This may seem to us an uninteresting passage, but to the Jew it would be a most impressive matter that the pedigree of Jesus could be traced back to Abraham.

It is further to be noted that this pedigree is most carefully arranged. It is arranged in three groups of fourteen people each. It is in fact what is technically known as a mnemonic, that is to say a thing so arranged that it is easy to memorize. It is always to be remembered that the Gospels were written hundreds of years before there was any such thing as a printed book. Very few people would be able to own actual copies of them, and so, if they wished to possess them, they would be compelled to memorize them. This pedigree, therefore, is arranged in such a way that it is easy to memorize. It is meant to prove that Jesus was the son of David, and is so arranged as to make it easy for people to carry it in their memories.

DECEMBER 21

The Three Stages

Matthew 1:1–17

This is the record of the lineage of Jesus Christ, the son of David, the son of Abraham.

Abraham begat Isaac, and Isaac begat Jacob. Jacob begat Judah and his brothers. Judah begat Phares and Zara, whose mother was Thamar. Phares begat Esrom. Esrom begat Aram. Aram begat Aminadab. Aminadab begat Naasson. Naasson begat Salmon. Salmon begat Booz, whose mother was Rachab. Booz begat Obed, whose mother was Ruth. Obed begat Jesse. Jesse begat David, the king.

David begat Solomon, whose mother was Uriah's wife. Solomon begat Roboam. Roboam begat Abia. Abia begat Asaph. Asaph begat Josaphat. Josaphat begat Joram. Joram begat Ozias. Ozias begat Joatham. Joatham begat Achaz. Achaz begat Ezekias. Ezekias begat Manasses. Manasses begat Amos. Amos begat Josias. Josias begat Jechonias, and his brothers, in the days when the exile to Babylon took place.

After the exile to Babylon Jechonias begat Salathiel. Salathiel begat Zorobabel. Zorobabel begat Abioud. Abioud begat Eliakim. Eliakim begat Azor. Azor begat Zadok. Zadok begat Acheim. Acheim begat Elioud. Elioud begat Eleazar. Eleazar begat Matthan. Matthan begat Jacob. Jacob begat Joseph, the husband of Mary, who was the mother of Jesus, who is called the Christ.

From Abraham to David there were in all fourteen generations. From David to the exile to Babylon there were also fourteen generations. From the exile to Babylon to the coming of Christ there were also fourteen generations.

There is something symbolic of the whole of human life in the way in which this pedigree is arranged. It is arranged in three sections, and the three sections are based on three great stages in Jewish history.

The first section takes the history down to David. David was the man who welded Israel into a nation, and made the Jews a power in the world. The first section takes the story down to the rise of Israel's greatest king.

The second section takes the story down to the exile to Babylon. It is the section which tells of the nation's shame, and tragedy, and disaster.

The third section takes the story down to Jesus Christ. Jesus Christ was the person who liberated men from their slavery, who rescued them from their disaster, and in whom the tragedy was turned into triumph.

These three sections stand for three stages in the spiritual history of mankind.

(i) *Man was born for greatness.* "God created man in His own image, in the image of God He created him" (Genesis 1:27). God said: "Let us make man in our image, after our likeness" (Genesis 1:26). Man was created in the image of God. God's dream for man was a dream of greatness. Man was designed for fellowship with God. He was created that he might be nothing less than kin to God. As Cicero, the Roman thinker, saw it, "the only difference between man and God is in point of time." Man was essentially man born to be king.

(ii) *Man lost his greatness.* Instead of being the servant of God, man became the slave of sin. As G. K. Chesterton said, "Whatever else is true of man, man is not what he was meant to be." He used his free-will to defy and to disobey God, rather than to enter into friendship and fellowship with him. Left to himself man had frustrated the design and plan of God in his creation.

(iii) *Man can regain his greatness.* Even then God did not abandon man to himself and to his own devices. God did not allow man to be destroyed by his own folly. The end of the story was not left to be tragedy. Into this world God sent his Son, Jesus Christ, that he might rescue man from the morass of sin in which he had lost himself, and liberate him from the chains of sin with which he had bound himself so that through him man might regain the fellowship with God which he had lost.

In his genealogy Matthew shows us the royalty of kingship gained; the tragedy of freedom lost; the glory of liberty restored. And that, in the mercy of God, is the story of mankind, and of each individual man.

DECEMBER 22

The Realization of Men's Dreams

Matthew 1:1–17

This is the record of the lineage of Jesus Christ, the son of David, the son of Abraham.

Abraham begat Isaac, and Isaac begat Jacob. Jacob begat Judah and his brothers. Judah begat Phares and Zara, whose mother was Thamar. Phares begat Esrom. Esrom begat Aram. Aram begat Aminadab. Aminadab begat Naasson. Naasson begat Salmon. Salmon begat Booz, whose mother was Rachab. Booz begat Obed, whose mother was Ruth. Obed begat Jesse. Jesse begat David, the king.

David begat Solomon, whose mother was Uriah's wife. Solomon begat Roboam. Roboam begat Abia. Abia begat Asaph. Asaph begat Josaphat. Josaphat begat Joram. Joram begat Ozias. Ozias begat Joatham. Joatham begat Achaz. Achaz begat Ezekias. Ezekias begat Manasses. Manasses begat Amos. Amos begat Josias. Josias begat Jechonias, and his brothers, in the days when the exile to Babylon took place.

After the exile to Babylon Jechonias begat Salathiel. Salathiel begat Zorobabel. Zorobabel begat Abioud. Abioud begat Eliakim. Eliakim begat Azor. Azor begat Zadok. Zadok begat Acheim. Acheim begat Elioud. Elioud begat Eleazar. Eleazar begat Matthan. Matthan begat Jacob. Jacob begat Joseph, the husband of Mary, who was the mother of Jesus, who is called the Christ.

From Abraham to David there were in all fourteen generations. From David to the exile to Babylon there were also fourteen generations. From the exile to Babylon to the coming of Christ there were also fourteen generations.

This passage stresses two special things about Jesus.

(i) It stresses the fact that he was the son of David. It was, indeed, mainly to prove this that the genealogy was composed. The New Testament stresses this again and again.

Peter states it in the first recorded sermon of the Christian Church (Acts 2:29–36). Paul speaks of Jesus Christ descended from David according to the flesh (Romans 1:3). The writer of the Pastoral Epistles urges men to remember that Jesus Christ, descended from David, was raised from the dead (2 Timothy 2:8). The writer of the Revelation hears the Risen Christ say: "I am the root and the offspring of David" (Revelation 22:16).

Repeatedly Jesus is so addressed in the Gospel story. After the healing of the blind and dumb man, the people exclaim, "Can this be the son of David?" (Matthew 12:23). The woman of Tyre and Sidon, who wished for Jesus' help for her daughter, calls him: "Son of David" (Matthew 15:22). The blind men cry out to Jesus as son of David (Matthew 20:30, 31). It is as son of David that the crowds greet Jesus when he enters Jerusalem for the last time (Matthew 21:9, 15).

There is something of great significance here. It is clear that it was the crowd, the common people, the ordinary folk, who addressed Jesus as son of David. The Jews were a waiting people. They never forgot, and never could forget, that they were the chosen people of God. Although their history was one long series of disasters, although at this very time they were a subject people, they never forgot their destiny. And it was the dream of the common people that into this world would come a descendant of David who would lead them to the glory which they believed to be theirs by right.

That is to say, Jesus is the answer to the dreams of men. It is true that so often men do not see it so. They see the answer to their dreams in power, in wealth, in material plenty, and in the realization of the ambitions which they cherish. But if ever men's dreams of peace and loveliness, and greatness and satisfaction, are to be realized, they can find their realization only in Jesus Christ.

Jesus Christ and the life he offers is the answer to the dreams of men. In the old Joseph story there is a text which goes far beyond the story itself. When Joseph was in prison, Pharaoh's chief butler and chief baker were prisoners along with him. They had their dreams, and their dreams troubled them, and their bewildered cry is, "We have had dreams, and there is no one to interpret them" (Genesis

40:8). Because man is man, because he is a child of eternity, man is always haunted by his dream; and the only way to the realization of it lies in Jesus Christ.

(ii) This passage also stresses that Jesus was the fulfillment of prophecy. In him the message of the prophets came true. We tend nowadays to make very little of prophecy. We are not really interested, for the most part, in searching for sayings in the Old Testament which are fulfilled in the New Testament. But prophecy does contain this great and eternal truth, that in this universe there is purpose and design and that God is meaning and willing certain things to happen.

J. H. Withers quotes a saying from Gerald Healy's play *The Black Stranger*. The scene is in Ireland, in the terrible days of famine in the mid-nineteenth century. For want of something better to do, and for lack of some other solution, the government had set men to digging roads to no purpose and to no destination. Michael finds out about this and comes home one day, and says in poignant wonder to his father, "They're makin' roads that lead to nowhere."

If we believe in prophecy that is what we can never say. History can never be a road that leads to nowhere. We may not use prophecy in the same way as our fathers did, but at the back of the fact of prophecy lies the eternal fact that life and the world are not on the way to nowhere, but on the way to the goal of God.

DECEMBER 23

Not the Righteous, but Sinners

Matthew 1:1–17

This is the record of the lineage of Jesus Christ, the son of David, the son of Abraham.

Abraham begat Isaac, and Isaac begat Jacob. Jacob begat Judah and his brothers. Judah begat Phares and Zara, whose mother was Thamar. Phares begat Esrom. Esrom begat Aram. Aram begat Aminadab. Aminadab begat Naasson. Naasson begat Salmon. Salmon begat Booz, whose mother was Rachab. Booz begat Obed, whose mother was Ruth. Obed begat Jesse. Jesse begat David, the king.

David begat Solomon, whose mother was Uriah's wife. Solomon begat Roboam. Roboam begat Abia. Abia begat Asaph. Asaph begat Josaphat. Josaphat begat Joram. Joram begat Ozias. Ozias begat Joatham. Joatham begat Achaz. Achaz begat Ezekias. Ezekias begat Manasses. Manasses begat Amos. Amos begat Josias. Josias begat Jechonias, and his brothers, in the days when the exile to Babylon took place.

After the exile to Babylon Jechonias begat Salathiel. Salathiel begat Zorobabel. Zorobabel begat Abioud. Abioud begat Eliakim. Eliakim begat Azor. Azor begat Zadok. Zadok begat Acheim. Acheim begat Elioud. Elioud begat Eleazar. Eleazar begat Matthan. Matthan begat Jacob. Jacob begat Joseph, the husband of Mary, who was the mother of Jesus, who is called the Christ.

From Abraham to David there were in all fourteen generations. From David to the exile to Babylon there were also fourteen generations. From the exile to Babylon to the coming of Christ there were also fourteen generations.

By far the most amazing thing about this pedigree is the names of the women who appear in it.

It is not normal to find the names of women in Jewish pedigrees at all. The woman had no legal rights; she was regarded, not as a person, but as a thing. She was merely the possession of her father or of her husband, and in his disposal to do with as he liked. In the regular form of morning prayer the Jew thanked God that he had not made him a Gentile, a slave, or a woman. The very existence of these names in any pedigree at all is a most surprising and extraordinary phenomenon.

But when we look at who these women were, and at what they did, the matter becomes even more amazing. Rachab, or as the Old Testament calls her, Rahab, was a harlot of Jericho (Joshua 2:1–7). Ruth was not even a Jewess; she was a Moabitess (Ruth 1:4), and does not the law itself lay it down, "No Ammonite or Moabite shall enter the assembly of the Lord; even to the tenth generation none belonging to them shall enter the assembly of the Lord for ever" (Deuteronomy 23:3)? Ruth belonged to an alien and a hated people. Tamar was a deliberate seducer and an adulteress (Genesis 38). Bathsheba, the mother of Solomon, was the woman whom David seduced from Uriah, her husband, with an unforgivable cruelty (2 Samuel 11 and 12). If Matthew had ransacked the pages of the Old Testament for improbable candidates he could not have discovered four more incredible ancestors for Jesus Christ. But, surely, there is something very lovely in this. Here, at the very beginning, Matthew shows us in symbol the essence of the gospel of God in Jesus Christ, for here he shows us the barriers going down.

(i) *The barrier between Jew and Gentile is down.* Rahab, the woman of Jericho, and Ruth, the woman of Moab, find their place within the pedigree of Jesus Christ. Already the great truth is there that in Christ there is neither Jew nor Greek. Here, at the very beginning, there is the universalism of the gospel and of the love of God.

(ii) *The barriers between male and female are down.* In no ordinary pedigree would the name of any woman be found; but such names are found in Jesus' pedigree. The old contempt is gone; and men and women stand equally dear to God, and equally important to his purposes.

(iii) *The barrier between saint and sinner is down.* Somehow God can use for his purposes, and fit into his scheme of things, those who have sinned greatly. "I came," said Jesus, "not to call the righteous, but sinners" (Matthew 9:13).

Here at the very beginning of the Gospel we are given a hint of the all-embracing width of the love of God. God can find his servants amongst those from whom the respectable orthodox would shudder away in horror.

DECEMBER 24

The Saviour's Entry into the World

Matthew 1:18–25
The birth of Jesus Christ happened in this way. Mary, His mother, was betrothed to Joseph, and, before they became man and wife, it was discovered that she was carrying a child in her womb through the action of the Holy Spirit. Although Joseph, her husband, was a man who kept the

law, he did not wish publicly to humiliate her, so he wished to divorce her secretly. When he was planning this, behold, an angel of the Lord came to him in a dream. "Joseph, son of David," said the angel, "do not hesitate to take Mary as your wife; for that which has been begotten within her has come from the Holy Spirit. She will bear a son, and you must call his name Jesus, for it is he who will save his people from their sins. All this happened that there might be fulfilled that which was spoken by the Lord through the prophet, 'Behold, the maiden will conceive and bear a son, and you must call his name Emmanuel, which is translated: God with us.'" So Joseph woke from his sleep, and did as the angel of the Lord had commanded him; and he accepted his wife, and he did not know her until she had borne a son; and he called his name Jesus.

To our Western ways of thinking the relationships in this passage are very bewildering. First, Joseph is said to be *betrothed* to Mary; then he is said to be planning quietly to *divorce* her; and then she is called his *wife*. But the relationships represent normal Jewish marriage procedure, in which there were three steps.

(i) There was the *engagement.* The engagement was often made when the couple were only children. It was usually made through the parents, or through a professional match-maker. And it was often made without the couple involved ever having seen each other. Marriage was held to be far too serious a step to be left to the dictates of the human heart.

(ii) There was the *betrothal.* The betrothal was what we might call the ratification of the engagement into which the couple had previously entered. At this point the engagement, entered into by the parents or the match-maker, could be broken if the girl was unwilling to go on with it. But once the betrothal was entered into, it was absolutely binding. It lasted for one year. During that year the couple were known as man and wife, although they had not the rights of man and wife. It could not be terminated in any other way than by divorce. In the Jewish law we frequently find what is to us a curious phrase. A girl whose fiance had died during the year of betrothal is called "a virgin who is a widow." It was at this stage that Joseph and Mary were.

They were betrothed, and if Joseph wished to end the betrothal, he could do so in no other way than by divorce; and in that year of betrothal Mary was legally known as his wife.

(iii) The third stage was *the marriage proper,* which took place at the end of the year of betrothal.

If we remember the normal Jewish wedding customs, then the relationships in this passage are perfectly usual and perfectly clear.

So at this stage it was told to Joseph that Mary was to bear a child, that that child had been begotten by the Holy Spirit, and that he must call the child by the name Jesus. *Jesus* is the Greek form of the Jewish name *Joshua,* and *Joshua* means *Jehovah is salvation.* Long ago the Psalmist had heard God say, "He will redeem Israel from all his iniquities" (Psalm 130:8). And Joseph was told that the child to be born would grow into the Saviour who would save God's people from their sins. Jesus was not so much the Man born to be King as the Man born to be Saviour. He came to this world, not for his own sake, but for men and for our salvation.

DECEMBER 25

Born of the Holy Spirit

Matthew 1:18–25

The birth of Jesus Christ happened in this way. Mary, His mother, was betrothed to Joseph, and, before they became man and wife, it was discovered that she was carrying a child in her womb through the action of the Holy Spirit. Although Joseph, her husband, was a man who kept the law, he did not wish publicly to humiliate her, so he wished to divorce her secretly. When he was planning this, behold, an angel of the Lord came to him in a dream. "Joseph, son of David," said the angel, "do not hesitate to take Mary as your wife; for that which has been begotten within her has come from the Holy Spirit. She will bear a son, and you must call his name Jesus, for it is he who will save his people from their sins. All this happened that there might be fulfilled that which was spoken by the Lord through the prophet, 'Behold, the maiden will conceive and bear a son, and you must call his name Emmanuel, which is translated: God with us.'" So Joseph woke from his sleep, and did as the angel of the Lord had commanded him; and he accepted his wife; and he did not know her until she had borne a son; and he called his name Jesus.

This passage tells us how Jesus was born by the action of the Holy Spirit. It tells us of what we call the Virgin Birth. This is a doctrine which presents us with many difficulties; and our church does not compel us to accept it in the literal and the physical sense. This is one of the doctrines on which the church says that we have full liberty to come to our own conclusion. At the moment we are concerned only to find out what this means for us.

If we come to this passage with fresh eyes, and read it as if we were reading it for the first time, we will find that what it stresses is not so much that Jesus was born of a woman who was a virgin, as that the birth of Jesus is the work of the Holy Spirit. "Mary was found to be with child of the Holy Spirit." "That which is conceived in her is of the Holy Spirit." It is as if these sentences were underlined, and printed large. That is what Matthew wishes to say to us in this passage. What then does it mean to say that in the birth of Jesus the Holy Spirit of God was specially operative? Let us leave aside all the doubtful and debatable things, and concentrate on that great truth, as Matthew would wish us to do.

In Jewish thought the Holy Spirit had certain very definite functions. We cannot bring to this passage the *Christian* idea of the Holy Spirit in all its fullness, because Joseph would know nothing about that. We must interpret it in the light of the Jewish idea of the Holy Spirit, for it is that idea that Joseph would inevitably bring to this message, for that was all he knew.

(i) According to the Jewish idea, *the Holy Spirit was the person who brought God's truth to men.* It was the Holy Spirit who taught the prophets what to say; it was the Holy Spirit who taught men of God what to do; it was the Holy Spirit who, throughout the ages and the generations, brought God's truth to men. So then, Jesus is the one person who brings God's truth to men.

Let us put it in another way. Jesus is the one person who can tell us what God is like, and what God means us to be. In him alone we see what God is and what man ought to be. Before Jesus came men had only vague and shadowy, and often quite wrong, ideas about God; they could only at best guess and grope; but Jesus could say, "He who has seen me has seen the Father" (John 14:9). In Jesus we see the love, the compassion, the mercy, the seeking heart, the purity of God as nowhere else in all this world. With the coming of Jesus the time of guessing is gone, and the time of certainty is come. Before Jesus came men did not really know what goodness was. In Jesus alone we see true manhood, true goodness, true obedience to the will of God. Jesus came to tell us the truth about God and the truth about ourselves.

(ii) The Jews believed that the Holy Spirit not only brought God's truth to men, but also *enabled men to recognize that truth when they saw it.* So then Jesus opens men's eyes to the truth. Men are blinded by their own ignorance; they are led astray by their own prejudices; their minds and eyes are darkened by their own sins and their own passions. Jesus can open our eyes until we are able to see the truth.

In one of William J. Locke's novels there is a picture of a woman who has any amount of money, and who has spent half a lifetime on a tour of the sights and picture galleries of the world. She is weary and bored. Then she meets a Frenchman who has little of this world's goods, but who has a wide knowledge and a great love of beauty. He comes with her, and in his company things are completely different. "I never knew what things were like," she said to him, "until you taught me how to look at them."

Life is quite different when Jesus teaches us how to look at things. When Jesus comes into our hearts, he opens our eyes to see things truly.

DECEMBER 26

Creation and Re-creation

Matthew 1:18–25 (continued)

The birth of Jesus Christ happened in this way. Mary, His mother, was betrothed to Joseph, and, before they became man and wife, it was dis-covered that she was carrying a child in her womb through the action of the Holy Spirit. Although Joseph, her husband, was a man who kept the law, he did not wish publicly to humiliate her, so he wished to divorce her secretly. When he was planning this, behold, an angel of the Lord came to him in a dream. "Joseph, son of David," said the angel, "do not hesitate to take Mary as your wife; for that which has been begotten within her has come from the Holy Spirit. She will bear a son, and you must call his name Jesus, for it is he who will save his people from their sins. All this happened that there might be fulfilled that which was spoken by the Lord through the prophet, 'Behold, the maiden will conceive and bear a son, and you must call his name Emmanuel, which is translated: God with us.'" So Joseph woke from his sleep, and did as the angel of the Lord had commanded him; and he accepted his wife; and he did not know her until she had borne a son; and he called his name Jesus.

(iii) The Jews specially *connected the Spirit of God with the work of creation.* It was through his Spirit that God performed his creating work. In the beginning the Spirit of God moved upon the face of the waters and chaos became a world (Genesis 1:2). "By the word of the Lord the heavens were made," said the Psalmist, "and all their host by the breath of his mouth" (Psalm 33:6). (Both in Hebrew, *ruach,* and in Greek, *pneuma,* the word for *breath* and *spirit* is the same word.) "When thou sendest forth thy Spirit, they are created" (Psalm 104:30). "The Spirit of God has made me," said Job, "and the breath of the Almighty gives me life" (Job 33:4).

The Spirit is the Creator of the World and the Giver of Life. So, then, in Jesus there came into the world God's life-giving and creating power. That power, which reduced the primal chaos to order, is come to bring order to our disordered life. That power, which breathed life into that in which there was no life, is come to breathe life into our weaknesses and frustrations. We could put it this way— we are not really alive until Jesus enters into our lives.

(iv) The Jews specially connected the Spirit, not only with the work of creation, but *with the work of re-creation.* Ezekiel draws his grim picture of the valley of dry bones. He goes on to tell how the dry bones came alive; and then he hears God say, "I will cause breath to enter you, and you shall live" (Ezekiel 37:1–14). The rabbis had a saying, "God said to Israel: 'In this world my Spirit has put wisdom in you, but in the future my Spirit will make you to live again.'" When men are dead in sin and in lethargy, it is the Spirit of God which can waken them to life anew.

So then, in Jesus there came to this world the power which can re-create life. He can bring to life again the soul which is dead in sin; he can revive again the ideals which have died; he can make strong again the will to goodness which has perished. He can renew life, when men have lost all that life means.

There is much more in this chapter than the crude fact that Jesus Christ was born of a virgin mother. The essence of Matthew's story is that in the birth of Jesus the Spirit of God was operative as never before in this world. It is the Spirit who brings God's truth to men; it is the Spirit who enables men to recognize that truth when they see it; it is the Spirit who was God's agent in the creation of the world; it is the Spirit who alone can re-create the human soul when it has lost the life it ought to have.

Jesus enables us to see what God is and what man ought to be; Jesus opens the eyes of our minds so that we can see the truth of God for us; Jesus is the creating power come amongst men; Jesus is the re-creating power which can release the souls of men from the death of sin.

The Consolation of Israel

DECEMBER 27

Journey to Bethlehem

Luke 2:1–7

In these days a decree went out from Caesar Augustus that a census should be taken of all the world. The census first took place when Quirinius was governor of Syria; and everyone went to enrol himself, each man to his own town. So Joseph went up from Galilee, from the town of Nazareth, to Judaea, to David's town, which is called Bethlehem, because he belonged to the house and the line of David, to enrol himself with Mary who was betrothed to him and she was with child. When they arrived there her time to bear the child was completed; and she bore her first-born son and wrapped him in swaddling clothes and laid him in a manger because there was no room for them in the place where they had meant to lodge.

In the Roman Empire periodical censuses were taken with the double object of assessing taxation and of discovering those who were liable for compulsory military service. The Jews were exempt from military service, and, therefore, in Palestine a census would be predominantly for taxation purposes. Regarding these censuses, we have definite information as to what happened in Egypt; and almost certainly what happened in Egypt happened in Syria, too, and Judaea was part of the province of Syria. The information we have comes from actual census documents written on papyrus and then discovered in the dust-heaps of Egyptian towns and villages and in the sands of the desert.

Such censuses were taken every fourteen years. And from A.D. 20 until about A.D. 270 we possess actual documents from every census taken. If the fourteen-year cycle held good in Syria this census must have been in 8 B.C. and that was the year in which Jesus was born. It may be that Luke has made one slight mistake. Quirinius did not actually become governor of Syria until A.D. 6; but he held an official post previously in those regions from 10 B.C. until 7 B.C., and it was during that first period that this census must have been taken.

Critics used to question the fact that every man had to go to his own city to be enrolled; but here is an actual government edict from Egypt:

> Gaius Vibius Maximus, Prefect of Egypt, orders: "Seeing that the time has come for the house-to-house census, it is necessary to compel all those who for any cause whatsoever are residing outside their districts to return to their own homes, that they may both carry out the regular order of the census, and may also diligently attend to the cultivation of their allotments."

If that was the case in Egypt, it may well be that in Judaea, where the old tribal ancestries still held good, men had to go to the headquarters of their tribe. Here is an instance where further knowledge has shown the accuracy of the New Testament.

The journey from Nazareth to Bethlehem was 80 miles. The accommodation for travellers was most primitive. The eastern khan was like a series of stalls opening off a common courtyard. Travellers brought their own food; all that the innkeeper provided was fodder for the animals and a fire to cook. The town was crowded and there was no room for Joseph and Mary. So it was in the common courtyard that Mary's child was born. Swaddling clothes consisted of a square of cloth with a long bandage-like strip coming diagonally off from one corner. The child was first wrapped in the square of cloth and then the long strip was wound round and round about him. The word translated *manger* means a place where animals feed; and therefore it can be either the stable or the manger which is meant.

That there was no room in the inn was symbolic of what was to happen to Jesus. The only place where there was room for him was on a cross. He sought an entry to the over-crowded hearts of men; he could not find it; and still his search—and his rejection—go on.

DECEMBER 28

Shepherds and Angels

Luke 2:8–20

In this country there were shepherds who were in the fields, keeping watch over their flock by night. An angel of the Lord appeared to them and the

*glory of the Lord shone round about them and they were much afraid.
The angel said to them, "Do not be afraid; for—look you—I am bringing you good news of great joy, which will be to every people, for to-day a
Saviour has been born for you, in David's town, who is Christ the Lord.
You will recognize him by this sign. You will find the babe wrapped in
swaddling clothes and laid in a manger." And suddenly with the angel
there was a crowd of heaven's host, praising God and saying, "In the highest heights glory to God; and on earth peace to the men whose welfare he
ever seeks." When the angels had left them and gone away to heaven, the
shepherds said to each other, "Come! Let us go across to Bethlehem and let
us see this thing which has happened which the Lord has made known to
us." So they hurried on and they discovered Mary and Joseph, and the
babe lying in a manger. When they had seen him they told everyone about
the word which had been spoken to them about this child; and all who
heard were amazed at what was told them by the shepherds. But Mary
stored up these things in her memory and in her heart kept wondering
what they meant. So the shepherds returned glorifying and praising God
for all that they had seen, just as it had been told to them.*

It is a wonderful thing that the story should tell that the first an-
nouncement of God came to some shepherds. Shepherds were despised by the orthodox good people of the day. They were quite
unable to keep the details of the ceremonial law; they could not observe all the meticulous hand-washings and rules and regulations.
Their flocks made far too constant demands on them; and so the orthodox looked down on them. It was to simple men of the fields that
God's message first came.

But these were in all likelihood very special shepherds. We have already seen how in the Temple, morning and evening, an unblemished
lamb was offered as a sacrifice to God. To see that the supply of perfect offerings was always available the Temple authorities had their
own private sheep flocks; and we know that these flocks were pastured
near Bethlehem. It is most likely that these shepherds were in charge
of the flocks from which the Temple offerings were chosen. It is a lovely
thought that the shepherds who looked after the Temple lambs were
the first to see the Lamb of God who takes away the sin of the world.

We have already seen that when a boy was born, the local musicians congregated at the house to greet him with simple music. Jesus was born in a stable in Bethlehem and therefore that ceremony could not be carried out. It is a lovely thought that the minstrelsy of heaven took the place of the minstrelsy of earth, and angels sang the songs for Jesus that the earthly singers could not sing.

All through these readings we must have been thinking of the rough simplicity of the birth of the Son of God. We might have expected that, if he had to be born into this world at all, it would be in a palace or a mansion. There was a European monarch who worried his court by often disappearing and walking incognito amongst his people. When he was asked not to do so for security's sake, he answered, "I cannot rule my people unless I know how they live." It is the great thought of the Christian faith that we have a God who knows the life we live because he too lived it and claimed no special advantage over common men.

DECEMBER 29

The Ancient Ceremonies Are Observed

Luke 2:21–24

When the eight days necessarily prior to circumcision had elapsed, he was called by the name of Jesus, the name by which he had been called by the angel before he had been conceived in the womb. When the time which, according to the law of Moses, must precede the ceremony of purification had elapsed, they brought him up to Jerusalem to present him to the Lord (in accordance with the regulation in the Lord's law, "Every male that opens the womb shall be called holy to the Lord") and to make the sacrifice which the regulation in the Lord's law lays down, that is, a pair of doves or two young pigeons.

In this passage we see Jesus undergoing three ancient ceremonies which every Jewish boy had to undergo.

(i) *Circumcision.* Every Jewish boy was circumcised on the eighth day after his birth. So sacred was that ceremony that it could be carried out even on a Sabbath when the law forbade almost every other act which was not absolutely essential; and on that day a boy received his name.

(ii) *The Redemption of the Firstborn.* According to the law (Exodus 13:2) every firstborn male, both of human beings and of cattle, was sacred to God. That law may have been a recognition of the gracious power of God in giving human life, or it may even have been a relic of the day when children were sacrificed to the gods. Clearly if it had been carried out literally life would have been disrupted. There was therefore a ceremony called the Redemption of the Firstborn (Numbers 18:16). It is laid down that for the sum of five shekels—approximately 75p—parents could, as it were, buy back their son from God. The sum had to be paid to the priests. It could not be paid sooner than thirty-one days after the birth of the child and it might not be long delayed after that.

(iii) *The Purification after Childbirth.* When a woman had borne a child, if it was a boy, she was unclean for forty days, if it was a girl, for eighty days. She could go about her household and her daily business but she could not enter the Temple or share in any religious ceremony (Leviticus 12). At the end of that time she had to bring to the Temple a lamb for a burnt offering and a young pigeon for a sin offering. That was a somewhat expensive sacrifice, and so the law laid it down (Leviticus 12:8) that if she could not afford the lamb she might bring another pigeon. The offering of the two pigeons instead of the lamb and the pigeon was technically called *the Offering of the Poor.* It was the offering of the poor which Mary brought. Again we see that it was into an ordinary home that Jesus was born, a home where there were no luxuries, a home where every penny had to be looked at twice, a home where the members of the family knew all about the difficulties of making a living and the haunting insecurity of life. When life is worrying for us we must remember that Jesus knew what the difficulties of making ends meet can be.

These three ceremonies are strange old ceremonies; but all three have at the back of them the conviction that a child is a gift of God. The Stoics used to say that a child was not *given* to a parent but only *lent.* Of all God's gifts there is none for which we shall be so answerable as the gift of a child.

DECEMBER 30

A Dream Realized

Luke 2:25–35

Now—look you—there was a man in Jerusalem called Simeon. This man was good and pious. He was waiting for the comforting of Israel and the Holy Spirit was upon him. He had received a message from the Holy Spirit that he would not see death until he had seen the Lord's Anointed One. So he came in the Spirit to the Temple precincts. When his parents brought in the child Jesus, to do regarding him the customary ceremonies laid down by the law, he took him into his arms and blessed God and said, "Now O Lord, as you said, let your servant depart in peace, because my eyes have seen your instrument of salvation, which you have prepared before all the people, a light to bring your revelation to the Gentiles, and the glory of your people Israel." His father and mother were amazed at what was said about him. Simeon blessed them and said to Mary his mother, "Look you, this child is appointed to be the cause whereby many in Israel will fall and many rise and for a sign which will meet with much opposition. As for you—a sword will pierce your soul—and all this will happen that the inner thoughts of many hearts may be revealed."

There was no Jew who did not regard his own nation as the chosen people. But the Jews saw quite clearly that by human means their nation could never attain to the supreme world greatness which they believed their destiny involved. By far the greater number of them believed that because the Jews were the chosen people they were bound some day to become masters of the world and lords of all the nations. To bring in that day some believed that some great, celestial champion would descend upon the earth; some believed that there would arise another king of David's line and that all the old glories would revive; some believed that God himself would break directly into history by supernatural means. But in contrast to all that there were some few people who were known as *the Quiet in the Land.* They had no dreams of violence and of power and of armies with banners; they believed in a life of constant prayer and quiet watchfulness until

God should come. All their lives they waited quietly and patiently upon God. Simeon was like that; in prayer, in worship, in humble and faithful expectation he was waiting for the day when God would comfort his people. God had promised him through the Holy Spirit that his life would not end before he had seen God's own Anointed King. In the baby Jesus he recognized that King and was glad. Now he was ready to depart in peace and his words have become the *Nunc Dimittis,* another of the great and precious hymns of the church.

In verse 34 Simeon gives a kind of summary of the work and fate of Jesus.

(i) He will be the cause whereby *many will fall.* This is a strange and a hard saying but it is true. It is not so much God who judges a man; a man judges himself; and his judgment is his reaction to Jesus Christ. If, when he is confronted with that goodness and that loveliness, his heart runs out in answering love, he is within the Kingdom. If, when so confronted, he remains coldly unmoved or actively hostile, he is condemned. There is a great refusal just as there is a great acceptance.

(ii) He will be the cause whereby *many will rise.* Long ago Seneca said that what men needed above all was a hand let down to lift them up. It is the hand of Jesus which lifts a man out of the old life and into the new, out of the sin into the goodness, out of the shame into the glory.

(iii) He will meet with *much opposition.* Towards Jesus Christ there can be no neutrality. We either surrender to him or are at war with him. And it is the tragedy of life that our pride often keeps us from making that surrender which leads to victory.

DECEMBER 31

A Lovely Old Age

Luke 2:36–40

There was a prophetess called Anna. She was the daughter of Phanuel and she belonged to the tribe of Asher. She was far advanced in years. She had lived with her husband ever since seven years after she came to womanhood; and now she was a widow of eighty-four years of age. She never left the Temple and day and night she worshipped with fastings and with prayers. At that very time she came up and she began to give thanks to God and she kept speaking about him to all those who were waiting expectantly for the deliverance of Jerusalem. When they had completed everything which the Lord's law lays down they returned to Galilee to their own town of Nazareth. And the child grew bigger and stronger and he was filled with wisdom, and God's grace was on him.

Anna, too, was one of the Quiet in the Land. We know nothing about her except what these verses tell but even in this brief compass Luke has drawn us a complete character sketch.

(i) Anna was a widow. *She had known sorrow and she had not grown bitter.* Sorrow can do one of two things to us. It can make us hard, bitter, resentful, rebellious against God. Or it can make us kinder, softer, more sympathetic. It can despoil us of our faith; or it can root faith ever deeper. It all depends how we think of God. If we think of him as a tyrant we will resent him. If we think of him as Father we too will be sure that

> A Father's hand will never cause
> His child a needless tear.

(ii) She was eighty-four years of age. *She was old and she had never ceased to hope.* Age can take away the bloom and the strength of our bodies; but age can do worse—the years can take away the life of our hearts until the hopes that once we cherished die and we become dully content and grimly resigned to things as they are. Again it all depends on how we think of God. If we think of him as distant and detached we may well despair; but if we think of him as intimately connected with life, as having his hand on the helm, we too will be sure that the best is yet to be and the years will never kill our hope.

How then was Anna such as she was?

(i) *She never ceased to worship.* She spent her life in God's house with God's people. God gave us his church to be our mother in the faith. We rob ourselves of a priceless treasure when we neglect to be one with his worshipping people.

(ii) *She never ceased to pray.* Public worship is great; but private worship is also great. As someone has truly said, "They pray best together who first pray alone." The years had left Anna without bitterness and in unshakable hope because day by day she kept her contact with him who is the source of strength and in whose strength our weakness is made perfect.

All Flesh Shall See the Salvation of God

JANUARY 1

The Birthplace of the King

Matthew 2:1–2

When Jesus was born in Bethlehem in Judaea, in the days of Herod the King, behold there came to Jerusalem wise men from the East. "Where," they said, "is the newly born King of the Jews? For we have seen his star in its rising and we have come to worship him."

It was in Bethlehem that Jesus was born. Bethlehem was quite a little town six miles to the south of Jerusalem. In the olden days it had been called Ephrath or Ephratah. The name *Bethlehem* means *The House of Bread,* and Bethlehem stood in a fertile countryside, which made its name a fitting name. It stood high up on a gray limestone ridge more than two thousand five hundred feet in height. The ridge had a summit at each end, and a hollow-like saddle between them. So, from its position, Bethlehem looked like a town set in an amphitheater of hills.

Bethlehem had a long history. It was there that Jacob had buried Rachel, and had set up a pillar of memory beside her grave (Genesis 48:7; 35:20). It was there that Ruth had lived when she married Boaz (Ruth 1:22), and from Bethlehem Ruth could see the land of Moab, her native land, across the Jordan valley. But above all Bethlehem was the home and the city of David (1 Samuel 16:1; 17:12; 20:6); and it was for the water of the well of Bethlehem that David longed when he was a hunted fugitive upon the hills (2 Samuel 23:14, 15).

In later days we read that Rehoboam fortified the town of Bethlehem (2 Chronicles 11:6). But in the history of Israel, and in the minds of the people, Bethlehem was uniquely the city of David. It was from the line of David that God was to send the great deliverer of his people. As the prophet Micah had it: "O Bethlehem Ephrathah, who are little to be among the clans of Judah, from you shall come forth for me one who is to be ruler in Israel, whose origin is from old, from ancient days" (Micah 5:2).

It was in Bethlehem, David's city, that the Jews expected great David's greater Son to be born; it was there that they expected God's Anointed One to come into the world. And it was so.

The picture of the stable and the manger as the birthplace of Jesus is a picture indelibly etched in our minds; but it may well be that that picture is not altogether correct. Justin Martyr, one of the greatest of the early fathers, who lived about A.D. 150, and who came from the district near Bethlehem, tells us that Jesus was born in a cave near the village of Bethlehem (Justin Martyr: *Dialogue with Trypho,* 78, 304); and it may well be that Justin's information is correct. The houses in Bethlehem are built on the slope of the limestone ridge; and it is very common for them to have a cave-like stable hollowed out in the limestone rock below the house itself; and very likely it was in such a cave-stable that Jesus was born.

To this day such a cave is shown in Bethlehem as the birthplace of Jesus and above it the Church of the Nativity has been built. For very long that cave has been shown as the birthplace of Jesus. It was so in the days of the Roman Emperor, Hadrian, for Hadrian, in a deliberate attempt to desecrate the place, erected a shrine to the heathen god Adonis above it. When the Roman Empire became Christian, early in the fourth century, the first Christian Emperor, Constantine, built a great church there, and that church, much altered and often restored, still stands.

H. V. Morton tells how he visited the Church of the Nativity in Bethlehem. He came to a great wall, and in the wall there was a door so low that he had to stoop to enter it; and through the door, and on the other side of the wall, there was the church. Beneath the high altar of the church is the cave, and when the pilgrim descends into it he finds a little cavern about fourteen yards long and four yards wide, lit by silver lamps. In the floor there is a star, and round it a Latin inscription: "Here Jesus Christ was born of the Virgin Mary."

When the Lord of Glory came to this earth, he was born in a cave where men sheltered the beasts. The cave in the Church of the Nativity in Bethlehem may be that same cave, or it may not be. That we will never know for certain. But there is something beautiful in the symbolism that the church where the cave is has a door so low that all must stoop to enter. It is supremely fitting that every man should approach the infant Jesus upon his knees.

JANUARY 2

The Homage of the East

Matthew 2:1–2

When Jesus was born in Bethlehem in Judaea, in the days of Herod the King, behold there came to Jerusalem wise men from the East. "Where," they said, "is the newly born King of the Jews? For we have seen his star in its rising and we have come to worship him."

When Jesus was born in Bethlehem there came to do him homage wise men from the East. The name given to these men is *Magi,* and that is a word which is difficult to translate. Herodotus (1:101, 132) has certain information about the Magi. He says that they were originally a Median tribe. The Medes were part of the Empire of the Persians. They tried to overthrow the Persians and substitute the power of the Medes. The attempt failed. From that time the Magi ceased to have any ambitions for power or prestige, and became a tribe of priests. They became in Persia almost exactly what the Levites were in Israel. They became the teachers and instructors of the Persian kings. In Persia no sacrifice could be offered unless one of the Magi was present. They became men of holiness and wisdom.

These Magi were men who were skilled in philosophy, medicine, and natural science. They were soothsayers and interpreters of dreams. In later times the word *Magus* developed a much lower meaning, and came to mean little more than a fortune-teller, a sorcerer, a magician, and a charlatan. Such was Elymas, the sorcerer (Acts 13: 6, 8), and Simon who is commonly called Simon Magus (Acts 8: 9, 11). But at their best the Magi were good and holy men, who sought for truth.

In those ancient days all men believed in astrology. They believed that they could foretell the future from the stars, and they believed that a man's destiny was settled by the star under which he was born. It is not difficult to see how that belief arose. The stars pursue their unvarying courses; they represent the order of the universe. If then there suddenly appeared some brilliant star, if the unvarying order of the heavens was broken by some special phenomenon, it did look as if God was breaking into his own order, and announcing some special thing.

We do not know what brilliant star those ancient Magi saw. Many suggestions have been made. About 11 B.C. Halley's comet was visible shooting brilliantly across the skies. About 7 B.C. there was a brilliant conjunction of Saturn and Jupiter. In the years 5 to 2 B.C. there was an unusual astronomical phenomenon. In those years, on the first day of the Egyptian month, Mesori, Sirius, the dog star, rose heliacally, that is at sunrise, and shone with extraordinary brilliance. Now the name *Mesori* means *the birth of a prince,* and to those ancient astrologers such a star would undoubtedly mean the birth of some great king. We cannot tell what star the Magi saw; but it was their profession to watch the heavens, and some heavenly brilliance spoke to them of the entry of a king into the world.

It may seem to us extraordinary that those men should set out from the East to find a king, but the strange thing is that, just about the time Jesus was born, there was in the world a strange feeling of expectation of the coming of a king. Even the Roman historians knew about this. Not so very much later than this Suetonius could write, "There had spread over all the Orient an old and established belief, that it was fated at that time for men coming from Judea to rule the world" (Suetonius: *Life of Vespasian,* 4:5). Tacitus tells of the same belief that "there was a firm persuasion that at this very time the East was to grow powerful, and rulers coming from Judea were to acquire universal empire" (Tacitus: *Histories,* 5:13). The Jews had the belief that "about that time one from their country should become governor of the habitable earth" (Josephus: *Wars of the Jews,* 6:5, 4). At a slightly later time we find Tiridates, King of Armenia, visiting Nero at Rome with his Magi along with him (Suetonius: *Life of Nero,* 13:1). We find the Magi in Athens sacrificing to the memory of Plato (Seneca: *Epistles,* 58:31). Almost at the same time as Jesus was born we find Augustus, the Roman Emperor, being hailed as the Savior of the World, and Virgil, the Roman poet, writing his Fourth Eclogue, which is known as the Messianic Eclogue, about the golden days to come.

There is not the slightest need to think that the story of the coming of the Magi to the cradle of Christ is only a lovely legend. It is exactly the kind of thing that could easily have happened in that ancient world. When Jesus Christ came the world was in an eagerness of expectation. Men were waiting for God and the desire for God was in their hearts. They had discovered that they could not build the golden age without God. It was to a waiting world that Jesus came; and, when he came, the ends of the earth were gathered at his cradle. It was the first sign and symbol of the world conquest of Christ.

JANUARY 3

The Crafty King

Matthew 2:3–9

When Herod the king heard of this he was disturbed, and so was all Jerusalem with him. So he collected all the chief priests and scribes of the people, and asked them where the Anointed One of God was to be born. They said to him, "In Bethlehem in Judaea. For so it stands written through the prophets. 'And you Bethlehem, land of Judah, are by no means the least among the leaders of Judah. For there shall come forth from you the leader, who will be a shepherd to my people Israel.'" Then Herod secretly summoned the wise men, and carefully questioned them about the time when the star appeared. He sent them to Bethlehem. "Go," he said, "and make every effort to find out about the little child. And, when you have found him, send news to me, that I, too, may come and worship him." When they had listened to the king they went on their way.

It came to the ears of Herod that the wise men had come from the East, and that they were searching for the little child who had been born to be King of the Jews. Any king would have been worried at the report that a child had been born who was to occupy his throne. But Herod was doubly disturbed.

Herod was half Jew and half Idumean. There was Edomite blood in his veins. He had made himself useful to the Romans in the wars and civil wars of Palestine, and they trusted him. He had been appointed governor in 47 B.C.; in 40 B.C. he had received the title of king; and he was to reign until 4 B.C. He had wielded power for long. He was called Herod the Great, and in many ways he deserved the title. He was the only ruler of Palestine who ever succeeded in keeping the peace and in bringing order into disorder. He was a great builder; he was indeed the builder of the Temple in Jerusalem. He could be generous. In times of difficulty he remitted the taxes to make things easier for the people; and in the famine of 25 B.C. he had actually melted down his own gold plate to buy corn for the starving people.

But Herod had one terrible flaw in his character. He was almost insanely suspicious. He had always been suspicious, and the older he became the more suspicious he grew, until, in his old age, he was, as someone said, "a murderous old man." If he suspected anyone as a rival to his power, that person was promptly eliminated. He murdered his wife Mariamne and her mother Alexandra. His eldest son, Antipater, and two other sons, Alexander and Aristobulus, were all assassinated by him. Augustus, the Roman Emperor, had said, bitterly, that it was safer to be Herod's pig than Herod's son. (The saying is even more epigrammatic in Greek, for in Greek *hus* is the word for a *pig,* and *huios* is the word for a *son.*)

Something of Herod's savage, bitter, warped nature can be seen from the provisions he made when death came near. When he was seventy he knew that he must die. He retired to Jericho, the loveliest of all his cities. He gave orders that a collection of the most distinguished citizens of Jerusalem should be arrested on trumped-up charges and imprisoned. And he ordered that the moment he died, they should all be killed. He said grimly that he was well aware that no one would mourn for his death, and that he was determined that some tears should be shed when he died.

It is clear how such a man would feel when news reached him that a child was born who was destined to be king. Herod was troubled, and Jerusalem was troubled, too, for Jerusalem well knew the steps that Herod would take to pin down this story and to eliminate this child. Jerusalem knew Herod, and Jerusalem shivered as it waited for his inevitable reaction.

Herod summoned the chief priests and the scribes. The scribes were the experts in scripture and in the law. The chief priests consisted of two kinds of people. They consisted of ex-high-priests. The high-priesthood was confined to a very few families. They were the priestly aristocracy, and the members of these select families were called the chief priests. So Herod summoned the religious aristocracy and the theological scholars of his day, and asked them where, according to the scriptures, the Anointed One of God should be born. They quoted the text in Micah 5:2 to him. Herod sent for the wise men, and dispatched them to make diligent search for the little child who had been born. He said that he, too, wished to come and worship the child; but his one desire was to murder the child born to be king.

No sooner was Jesus born than we see men grouping themselves into the three groups in which men are always to be found in regard to Jesus Christ. Let us look at the three reactions.

(i) There was the reaction of Herod, *the reaction of hatred and hostility.* Herod was afraid that this little child was going to interfere with his life, his place, his power, his influence, and therefore his first instinct was to destroy him.

There are still those who would gladly destroy Jesus Christ, because they see in him the one who interferes with their lives. They wish to do what they like, and Christ will not let them do what they like; and so they would kill him. The man whose one desire is to do what he likes has never any use for Jesus Christ. The Christian is the man who has ceased to do what he likes, and has dedicated his life to do as Christ likes.

(ii) There was the reaction of the chief priests and scribes, *the reaction of complete indifference.* It did not make the slightest difference to them. They were so engrossed in their Temple ritual and their legal discussions that they completely disregarded Jesus. He meant nothing to them.

There are still those who are so interested in their own affairs that Jesus Christ means nothing to them. The prophet's poignant question can still be asked: "Is it nothing to you, all you who pass by?" (Lamentations 1:12).

(iii) There was the reaction of the wise men, *the reaction of adoring worship,* the desire to lay at the feet of Jesus Christ the noblest gifts which they could bring.

Surely, when any man realizes the love of God in Jesus Christ, he, too, should be lost in wonder, love, and praise.

JANUARY 4

Gifts for Christ

Matthew 2:9–12

And, behold, the star, which they had seen in its rising, led them on until it came and stood over the place where the little child was. When they saw the star, they rejoiced with exceeding great joy. When they came into the house, they saw the little child with Mary, his mother, and they fell down and worshipped him; and they opened their treasures, and offered to him gifts, gold, frankincense and myrrh. And because a message from God came to them in a dream, telling them not to go back to Herod, they returned to their own country by another way.

So the wise men found their way to Bethlehem. We need not think that the star literally moved like a guide across the sky. There is poetry here, and we must not turn lovely poetry into crude and lifeless prose. But over Bethlehem the star was shining. There is a lovely legend which tells how the star, its work of guidance completed, fell into the well at Bethlehem, and that it is still there and can still be seen sometimes by those whose hearts are pure.

Later legends have been busy with the wise men. In the early days Eastern tradition said that there were twelve of them. But now the tradition that there were three is almost universal. The New Testament does not say that there were three, but the idea that there were three no doubt arose from the threefold gift which they brought.

Later legend made them kings. And still later legend gave them names, Casper, Melchior and Balthasar. Still later legend assigned to each a personal description, and distinguished the gift which each of them gave to Jesus. Melchior was an old man, gray haired, and with a long beard, and it was he who brought the gift of gold. Caspar was young and beardless, and ruddy in countenance, and it was he who brought the gift of frankincense. Balthasar was swarthy, with the beard newly grown upon him, and it was he who brought the gift of myrrh.

From very early times men have seen a peculiar fitness in the gifts the wise men brought. They have seen in each gift something which specially matched some characteristic of Jesus and his work.

(i) *Gold is the gift for a king.* Seneca tells us that in Parthia it was the custom that no one could ever approach the king without a gift. And gold, the king of metals, is the fit gift for king of men.

So then Jesus was "the Man born to be King." But he was to reign, not by force, but by love; and he was to rule over men's hearts, not from a throne, but from a cross.

We do well to remember that Jesus Christ is King. We can never meet Jesus on an equality. We must always meet him on terms of complete submission. Nelson, the great admiral, always treated his vanquished opponents with the greatest kindness and courtesy. After one of his naval victories, the defeated admiral was brought aboard Nelson's flagship and on to Nelson's quarter-deck. Knowing Nelson's reputation for courtesy, and thinking to trade upon it, he advanced across the quarter-deck with hand outstretched as if he was advancing to shake hands with an equal. Nelson's hand remained by his side. "Your sword first," he said, "and then your hand." Before we must be friends with Christ, we must submit to Christ.

(ii) *Frankincense is the gift for a priest.* It was in the Temple worship and at the Temple sacrifices that the sweet perfume of frankincense was used. The function of a priest is to open the way to God for men. The Latin word for priest is *pontifex,* which means a *bridge-builder.* The priest is the man who builds a bridge between men and God.

That is what Jesus did. He opened the way to God; he made it possible for men to enter into the very presence of God.

(iii) *Myrrh is the gift for one who is to die.* Myrrh was used to embalm the bodies of the dead.

Jesus came into the world to die. Holman Hunt has a famous picture of Jesus. It shows Jesus at the door of the carpenter's shop in Nazareth. He is still only a boy and has come to the door to stretch his limbs which had grown cramped over the bench. He stands there in the doorway with arms outstretched, and behind him, on the wall, the setting sun throws his shadow, and it is the shadow of a cross. In the background there stands Mary, and as she sees that shadow there is the fear of coming tragedy in her eyes.

Jesus came into the world to live for men, and, in the end, to die for men. He came to give for men his life and his death.

Gold for a king, frankincense for a priest, myrrh for one who was to die—these were the gifts of the wise men, and, even at the cradle of Christ, they foretold that he was to be the true King, the perfect High-Priest, and in the end the supreme Saviour of men.

JANUARY 5

The Dawning Realization

Luke 2:41–52

Every year his parents used to go to Jerusalem for the feast of the Passover. When he was twelve years of age, they went up according to the custom of the feast, and when they had completed the days of the feast and returned home, the child Jesus stayed on in Jerusalem. His parents were not aware of this. They thought he was in the caravan and when they had gone a day's journey they looked for him amongst their kinsfolk and acquaintances. When they did not find him they turned back to Jerusalem, looking for him all the time. After three days they found him in the Temple precincts, sitting in the middle of the rabbis, listening to them and asking them questions. All who were listening were astonished at his understanding and at his answers. When they saw him they were amazed. His mother said to him, "Child, why did you do this to us? Look you, your father and I have been looking for you and we have been very worried." He said to them, "Why were you looking for me? Did you not know that I was bound to be in my Father's house?" They did not understand the meaning of what he said to them. So he came home with them and went to Nazareth and he was obedient to them. His mother kept all these things in her heart. And Jesus grew wise and grew bigger and increased in favour with God and man.

This is a supremely important passage in the Gospel story. It was laid down by law that every adult male Jew who lived within fifteen miles of Jerusalem must attend the Passover. In point of fact it was the aim of every Jew in all the world at least once in a lifetime to attend that feast.

A Jewish boy became a man when he was twelve years of age. Then he became *a son* of the law and had to take the obligations of the law upon him. So at twelve Jesus for the first time went to the Passover. We may well imagine how the holy city and the Temple and the sacred ritual fascinated him.

When his parents returned he lingered behind. It was not through carelessness that they did not miss him. Usually the women in a caravan started out much earlier than the men for they travelled more slowly. The men started later and travelled faster and the two sections would not meet until the evening encampment was reached. It was Jesus' first Passover. No doubt Joseph thought he was with Mary; Mary thought that he was with Joseph, and not till the evening camp did they miss him.

They returned to Jerusalem to search for him. For the Passover season it was the custom for the Sanhedrin to meet in public in the Temple court to discuss, in the presence of all who would listen, religious and theological questions. It was there they found Jesus. We must not think of it as a scene where a precocious boy was dominating a crowd of his seniors. *Hearing and asking questions* is the regular Jewish phrase for a student learning from his teachers. Jesus was listening to the discussions and eagerly searching for knowledge like an avid student.

And now comes one of the key passages in the life of Jesus. "*Your father* and I," said Mary, "have been looking for you anxiously." "Did you not know," said Jesus, "that I must be in *my Father's* house?" See how very gently but very definitely Jesus takes the name *father* from Joseph and gives it to God. At some time Jesus must have discovered his own unique relationship to God. He cannot have known it when he was a child in the manger and a baby at his mother's breast or he would be a monstrosity. As the years went on he must have had thoughts; and then at this first Passover, with manhood dawning, there came in a sudden blaze of realization the consciousness that he was in a unique sense the Son of God.

Here we have the story of the day when Jesus discovered who he was. And mark this—the discovery did not make him proud. It did not make him look down on his humble parents, the gentle Mary and the hard-working Joseph. He went home and *he was obedient to them.* The fact that he was God's Son made him the perfect son of his human parents. The real man of God does not despise earthly ties; just because he is God's man he discharges human duties with supreme fidelity.

JANUARY 6

The Courier of the King

Luke 3:1–6

In the fifteenth year of the reign of Tiberius Caesar, when Pontius Pilate was governor of Judaea, and when Herod was tetrarch of Galilee, his brother Philip tetrarch of Ituraea and the district of Trachonitis, and Lysanias tetrarch of Abilene, in the high-priesthood of Annas and Caiaphas, the word of God came to John, the son of Zacharias, when he was in the desert. So he came into the territory around Jordan, preaching a baptism of repentance whereby sins might be forgiven—as it stands written in the book of the words of Isaiah, the prophet, "The voice of one crying in the wilderness, 'Get ready the road of the Lord, make his paths straight; every ravine shall be filled up; every mountain and hill will be made low; the twisted places will be made into straight roads and the rough places into smooth; and all flesh shall see God's instrument of salvation.'"

To Luke the emergence of John the Baptist was one of the hinges on which history turned. So much so is that the case that he dates it in no fewer than six different ways.

(i) Tiberius was the successor of Augustus and therefore the second of the Roman emperors. As early as A.D. 11 or 12 Augustus had made him his colleague in the imperial power but he did not become sole emperor until A.D. 14. The fifteenth year of his reign would therefore be A.D. 28–29. Luke begins by setting the emergence of John against a world background, the background of the Roman Empire.

(ii) The next three dates Luke gives are connected with the political organization of Palestine. The title tetrarch literally means *governor of a fourth part*. In such provinces as Thessaly and Galatia, which were divided into four sections or areas, the governor of each part was known as a tetrarch; but later the word widened its meaning and came to mean the governor of any part. Herod the Great died in 4 B.C. after the reign of about forty years. He divided his kingdom between three of his sons and in the first instance the Romans approved the decision.

(*a*) To Herod Antipas were left Galilee and Peraea. He reigned from 4 B.C. to A.D. 39 and therefore Jesus' life was lived in Herod's reign and very largely in Herod's dominions in Galilee.

(*b*) To Herod Philip were left Ituraea and Trachonitis. He reigned from 4 B.C. to A.D. 33. Caesarea Philippi was called after him and was actually built by him.

(*c*) To Archelaus were left Judaea, Samaria, and Edom. He was a thoroughly bad king. The Jews in the end actually petitioned Rome for his removal; and Rome, impatient of the continual troubles in Judaea, installed a procurator or governor. That is how the Romans came directly to rule Judaea. At this time Pilate, who was in power from A.D. 25 until A.D. 37, was the Roman governor. So in this one sentence Luke gives us a panoramic view of the division of the kingdom which had once belonged to Herod the Great.

(iii) Of Lysanias we know practically nothing.

(iv) Having dealt with the world situation and the Palestinian political situation, Luke turns to the religious situation and dates John's emergence as being in the priesthood of Annas and Caiaphas. There never at any time were two high-priests at the one time. What then does Luke mean by giving these two names? The high-priest was at one and the same time the civil and the religious head of the community. In the old days the office of high-priest had been hereditary and for life. But with the coming of the Romans the office was the object of all kinds of intrigue. The result was that between 37 B.C. and A.D. 26 there were no fewer than twenty-eight different high-priests. Now Annas was actually high-priest from A.D. 7 until A.D. 14. He was therefore at this time out of office; but he was succeeded by no fewer than four of his sons and Caiaphas was his son-in-law. Therefore, although Caiaphas was the reigning high-priest, Annas was the power behind the throne. That is in fact why Jesus was brought first to him after his arrest (John 18:13) although at that time he was not in office. Luke associates his name with Caiaphas because, although Caiaphas was the actual high-priest, Annas was still the most influential priestly figure in the land.

Verses 4–6 are a quotation from Isaiah 40:3–5. When a king proposed to tour a part of his dominions in the east, he sent a courier before him to tell the people to prepare the roads. So John is regarded as the courier of the King. But the preparation on which he insisted was a preparation of heart and of life. "The King is coming," he said. "Mend, not your roads, but your lives." There is laid on everyone of us the duty to make life fit for the King to see.